COOPERATIVE LEARNING FOR INTERCULTURAL CLASSROOMS

T0377742

Cooperative Learning for Intercultural Classrooms helps both pre-service and in-service teachers to develop a well-researched pedagogy that supports inclusive practice for a globalised world. It provides: an overview of theoretical perspectives that illustrate why cooperative learning is an effective learning strategy; reviews research findings about how cooperative learning supports inclusion; and outlines the strategies and methods that support teachers in putting cooperative learning into practice.

Providing a step-by-step guide to implementing cooperative learning for schools, teachers and teacher educators, this invaluable resource includes:

- guidelines for a staged approach to implementation;
- case studies of cooperative learning in classrooms from a range of different contexts, including Australia, England, Sweden, Italy, India, Singapore and Hong Kong;
- guidance on developing an effective professional development programme for a school;
- appendices with valuable information on a range of cooperative learning structures and explanations of the main types of cooperative learning used in classrooms.

Kate Ferguson-Patrick gained 15 years' experience teaching in primary settings in the UK and Australia before working at the University of Newcastle, Australia, as a primary curriculum and pedagogy specialist. Her long-term study of cooperative learning with early career teachers, developing professional development through action research, showed how this approach leads to democracy classrooms. She has published extensively on cooperative learning.

Wendy Jolliffe is Professor of Education and was, until recently, Head of Teacher Education at the University of Hull in the UK. She has worked as a deputy head-teacher in a primary school as well as nationally, advising universities on effective provision. She has published extensively on cooperative learning and is a board member of the International Association for the Study of Cooperation in Education (IASCE).

COOPERATIVE LEARNING FOR INTERCULTURAL CLASSROOMS

Case Studies for Inclusive Pedagogy

Kate Ferguson-Patrick and Wendy Jolliffe

Routledge
Taylor & Francis Group

LONDON AND NEW YORK

First published 2018
by Routledge
2 Park Square, Milton Park, Abingdon, Oxon OX14 4RN

and by Routledge
711 Third Avenue, New York, NY 10017

Routledge is an imprint of the Taylor & Francis Group, an informa business

British Library Cataloguing in Publication Data
A catalogue record for this book is available from the British Library

Library of Congress Cataloging in Publication Data
Names: Ferguson-Patrick, Kate, author. | Jolliffe, Wendy, author.
Title: Cooperative learning for intercultural classrooms : case studies for inclusive pedagogy / Kate Ferguson-Patrick and Wendy Jolliffe.
Description: Abingdon, Oxon ; New York, NY : Routledge, 2018. | Includes bibliographical references.
Identifiers: LCCN 2017048542| ISBN 9780815349440 (hardback) | ISBN 9780815349471 (pbk.) | ISBN 9781351164641 (ebook)
Subjects: LCSH: Group work in education—Case studies. | Motivation in education—Case studies. | Interaction analysis in education—Case studies. | Intercultural communication—Study and teaching—Case studies. | Multicultural education—Case studies.
Classification: LCC LB1032 .F37 2018 | DDC 370.117—dc23
LC record available at https://lccn.loc.gov/2017048542

ISBN: 978-0-8153-4944-0 (hbk)
ISBN: 978-0-8153-4947-1 (pbk)
ISBN: 978-1-351-16464-1 (ebk)

Typeset in Bembo
by Swales & Willis Ltd, Exeter, Devon, UK

CONTENTS

ACKNOWLEDGEMENTS

We would like to sincerely thank all contributors to the case studies – especially the teachers, students and other staff for their cooperation.

In particular, we would like to thank the teachers, students, other staff and management at:

- Boothferry Primary School, Goole, England;
- Lipson Co-operative Academy School, England;
- Fäladsskolan and Delfinskolan schools, Sweden;
- Västerholms School, Friskola, Sweden.
- Lok Sin Tong Leung Wong Wai Fong Memorial School, Hong Kong;
- Charlton Christian College, Australia;
- Urapunga School, Australia;
- Ankur Vidyamandir school in Pune city of the Maharashtra state, India.

We are also indebted to the following academic and teaching staff:

- Dr Sharon Ahlquist, Kristianstad University, Sweden;
- Dr Kam Wing Chan, Adjunct Assistant Professor, Department of Curriculum and Instruction, The Education University of Hong Kong;
- Lalita Agashe, Facilitator for teachers' professional development, including cooperative learning, India;
- Madhuri Deshpande, Managing Trustee of COER, India;
- Bryan John Lucas, percussion music teacher, Singapore;
- Dr Isabella Pescarmona, Lecturer at the University of Turin, Italy.

INTRODUCTION

This chapter will explore two key aspects that are fundamental to understanding how cooperative learning supports the intercultural classroom:

1. What is cooperative learning and why is it important to support 21st century teaching in a globalised world?
2. How does cooperative learning support inclusive learning for all?

This chapter will also provide an overview of the contents of the book and its central aim to support teachers to implement this inclusive pedagogy in the classroom.

Cooperative learning: an inclusive 21st century pedagogy

Collaboration and cooperation

Cooperative learning and **collaborative learning** are often used interchangeably in schools and there is some confusion among teachers about the terms. Some authors do distinguish between the two, and others do not. Collaborative learning has been defined as mutual engagement between members in a group when they try to solve a problem together (Dillenbourg et al., 1996), with equality also being cited as an important dimension (Damon and Phelps, 1989). Collaborative learning has also been defined as a term used to describe situations when joint intellectual efforts are required, with students working in groups larger than two and working on developing understandings as a team (Smith and MacGregor, 1992). Williams and Sheridan (2006) claimed that a shared interest is important when developing collaboration, while Bruner (1996) argued that collaboration implies student proactiveness and interaction in learning – although not in any particular manner.

In cooperative learning, students have specific sub-tasks and then need to reassemble these tasks to meet the common goal, whereas in collaborative learning partners or groups do the work together. Some subtle division of tasks can occur, with one partner taking on certain portions of the task and another taking on more strategic parts. However, as Dillenbourg (1999) noted, true collaborative learning requires a shifting of roles and of layers required in a task requiring high level reasoning as the layers are tightly interwoven. This is in contrast to cooperative learning, where division of sub-tasks is often decided at the beginning of the task and as a result the fixed division of these sub-tasks makes the task more stable. It is this level of complex thinking and working that children accomplish, once they have been taught explicitly how to cooperate. Therefore, once the teacher has scaffolded the collaboration through cooperative learning, the intention is that in time the students will collaborate without such teacher intervention.

One of the underlying differences between collaborative and cooperative learning relates to two different epistemological perspectives (Brody and Davidson, 1998). Cooperative learning has evolved from the work of Lewin (1946), centred on group dynamics and developed by the work of social psychologists, such as Johnson and Johnson (1975), Schmuck and Schmuck (2001) and Sharan (1990), into a theory of social interdependence. Collaborative learning's roots lie in constructivism (Kelly, 1955; Rorty, 1979; Vygotsky, 1978), along with the work of Britton (1970), who encouraged the creation of a community of learners with a focus on dialogue to support learning. This standpoint broadly rejects structure and is a philosophy of interaction. In contrast, cooperative learning focuses on group interaction through careful consideration of group dynamics. This has led to the identification of factors that are important in ensuring genuine cooperative learning. Chapter 1 explores these factors in depth, but it is important to note that according to Johnson and Johnson (2000), Slavin (1995b) and Kagan (1994), two aspects are particularly essential: **positive interdependence** and **individual accountability**. Positive interdependence exists when individuals understand that they cannot succeed unless everyone in the group succeeds and tasks are designed to facilitate this. Linked to this is the necessity for individual accountability, where each member of the group must be accountable for their share of the work. Johnson and Johnson (1999:73) summarise cooperative learning as, 'the instructional use of small groups in which pupils work together to maximise their own and each other's learning'.

Twenty-first century pedagogy implies a new way of learning and teaching; a way that assists and enhances a different set of beliefs and theories more appropriate for a new century – a globalised century. The notion of 21st century pedagogy, as opposed to previous century pedagogy, does continue to provoke debate but there is some consensus that students of current educational institutions, 'will need to function well in the globalized world in terms of competition for opportunities and collaboration with individuals from different cultures' (Zhao, 2010:429). As a result of global capitalism and globalisation, our 21st century students need to be interconnected and interdependent to address the global issues that have arisen, such as human rights abuses (Abdullahi, 2011; Cogan and Grossman, 2009).

We need to be aware of more reflective and critical pedagogies and curricula when focusing on issues around how we learn to live together in a globally interconnected world (Starkey, 2012).

Intercultural education is needed throughout the world to prepare students for a future in a culturally diverse world. This is particularly the case in Australia, which has a unique history that has shaped the diversity of its peoples, their cultures and lifestyles today. Three major contributors to Australia's demographic make-up are a diverse indigenous population, a British colonial past and extensive immigration from many different countries and cultures. Today, Australia's population of about 23 million is one of the most culturally and linguistically diverse populations in the world (NSW Department of Education, 2016).

Teaching for the 21st century should enable our students to learn to address key challenges facing this increasingly globalised world. Globalisation denotes increased interdependence in many areas of life; constant changes in national states and influential groups in the world; and, 'the growing moral sense of "oneness" transcending national borders' (Fujikane, 2003:143). Globalisation in schooling can influence developing citizens committed to social justice focusing particularly on intercultural competence, education for sustainability, skills for cooperation and collaboration and an emphasis on building attitudes and dispositions which link, rather than compete with, others. Many of the latter are non-academic outcomes of schooling, including beliefs, norms, values, motivation and behaviours (Ladwig, 2010). Education for the 21st century will focus on allowing students to move between workplaces and develop the metacognitive skills necessary to do this well. These include not simply memorisation and repetition, but include social skills and attitude sets. The Organisation for Economic Co-operation and Development (OECD) has formulated its own version of 21st century skills and competences through the Definition and Selection of Competences (DeSeCo) initiative, which also underpins the OECD Programme for International Student Assessment (PISA) (Ananiadou and Claro, 2009). The skills summarised are: collaboration; communication; creativity and innovation; critical thinking and problem solving; learning to learn; ICT literacy; flexibility, adaptability and initiative; and global awareness and citizenship. These are the skills we will relate to in the book when referring to 21st century skills. Please see Shear et al. (2010) and https://education.microsoft.com/GetTrained/ITL-Research for more information about these 21st century skills.

Intercultural competence

Intercultural competence is an important 21st century capability where, "intercultural competenc[i]es obviously play an integral role in learning to live together" (United Nations Economic Scientific and Cultural Organization [UNESCO], 2013:8). Deardorff (2006:247) claims the definition of intercultural competence, and the most often cited, is, 'the ability to communicate effectively and appropriately in intercultural situations'. Perry and Southwell (2011) pointed out that intercultural competence requires behaviour and communication, in addition to understanding, in relation to intercultural education. Behaviours that encourage communication between 'others' are essential. The ongoing refugee crises around the world also make intercultural competence such a crucial issue in many schools. Portera (2008:484) provides a good summary of the developments of intercultural education in Europe, claiming:

> Today, 'intercultural education' and 'intercultural pedagogy' are regarded as a more appropriate response to the new context of globalisation and the increasing convergence of different languages, religions, cultural behaviour and ways of thinking . . . For the first time in the history of pedagogy, children of immigrants were no longer regarded as a 'problem' or 'risk', but as 'resources'.

Portera and Grant (2017) highlight the urgency for more effective intercultural education and competences for a globalised world and have produced a summary of the competencies needed, which includes the ability to work in a cooperative group. Collaboration, implementing contextually appropriate behaviour (whether through words or actions), participating in meaningful interactions and relationships effectively and appropriately with people of different cultures to oneself and using skills of dialogue and negotiation in these contexts, is essential for intercultural competence.

It is also crucial that teachers are culturally responsive (Aronson and Laughter, 2015) and for this skill to be developed by students it must first be understood by teachers, who, 'need to know how to foster cultural competence, emotional awareness, and leadership skills to facilitate not just interactions, but meaningful interactions and relationships' (Kereluik et al., 2013:133). Teachers will need access to resources utilising skills of higher order thinking – for themselves and their students – and the use of culturally relevant or culturally responsive pedagogy (Ananiadou and Claro, 2009; Gay, 2000; Merryfield, 1998; Morrison et al., 2008).

What is culturally responsive pedagogy?

Previous doctoral research completed in 2014 showed that when teachers used cooperative learning, it led to a particular classroom ambience, in this case a 'democracy stance', and transformed classroom quality (Ferguson-Patrick, 2014). Democracy classrooms are classrooms that use inclusive pedagogies that increase participation and decrease exclusion (Florian and Black-Hawkins, 2011) such as cooperative learning, which is an example of inclusive pedagogy. Teachers in democracy classrooms are able to respect and respond to human differences in ways that include learners in daily classroom life (Florian and Black-Hawkins, 2011). Trusting relationships (Ferguson-Patrick, 2008) are built in these classrooms and improved relationships also lead to students with high self-esteem (Slavin, 1987). Cooperative learning is a pedagogy that teaches students how to respect and support each other, how to value and welcome difference and diversity; a pedagogy where all students are applauded for having a voice – an important factor in both a democratic society and an increasingly globalised world. The pedagogies selected by teachers who have high expectations of all students should be intellectually demanding (Mills and Gale, 2010) and should support students to respect diversity and value all, to develop a sense of responsible citizenship and be, 'focused on creating socially supportive and inclusive learning environments where students are positioned with autonomy' (Lingard and Keddie, 2013:429).

Cooperative learning activities provide a kind of 'learning laboratory' for students, to help a commitment to fairness, social responsibility and a concern for others. It can help to meet the needs of marginalised groups and build social bridges between diverse students (Schul, 2011). Encouraging equity and mutual engagement between members in a problem-solving group, cooperative learning also requires members to explain their understandings, experience different points of view that challenge their own and resolve differences in social cognitions and shared meanings. It requires a culture of listening and speaking to others about ideas and conflicts: vital in our increasingly diverse classrooms (Ferguson-Patrick, 2014). In 2006, the UNESCO Guidelines on Intercultural Education (UNESCO, 2006) argued that the guiding principles for intercultural education included the need to respect the cultural identity of the learners, and to provide all learners with the knowledge, skills and attitudes that allow respect and understanding between all groups in society. Cooperative learning is the key to preparing our students for the globalised world and a key culturally responsive pedagogy.

Research into cooperative learning

Before the 1970s all reported studies of cooperative learning had been conducted in college classrooms or in laboratories, using college students. After this, the research into cooperative learning grew as it concentrated on primary and secondary classroom research. From the late 1970s research into cooperative learning included Aronson's work on Jigsaw (Aronson et al., 1978); Shlomo and Yael Sharan's group investigation procedures (Sharan and Sharan, 1976); Kagan's cooperative structures in the 1980s (Kagan, 1989); and Cohen's research into complex instruction in 1986 at Stamford University in the USA (Cohen, 1986). Johnson and Johnson, as well as Sharan and Slavin, continued to develop ideas about cooperative learning in the 1980s, but theories about which were the most effective methods caused some debate. Johnson and Johnson's later work (Johnson and Johnson, 1975, 1999, 2005; Johnson, 1984; Johnson et al., 2000a) have clearly contributed to the more recent research into cooperative learning. Social interdependence theorists such as Johnson and Johnson asserted that the effects of cooperative learning are largely dependent on the cohesiveness of the group, whereas behaviourist-focused researchers, such as Slavin, claimed that its effectiveness was a result of a focus on the reward or goal structure under which students operated.

Johnson and Johnson are two of the most well-known researchers and advocates of cooperative learning at the present time. They pointed out that much research into the area of group dynamics disappeared in the 1950s, due to an emphasis on the individual in education. This re-appeared again in the 1970s with the emergence of more extensive research into the benefits of cooperative learning for overall student achievement in comparison with student achievement when working either individually or competitively. It was in 1979 that the first International Association for the Study of Cooperation in Education (IASCE) conference occurred in Israel, as a result of the interest in group work at this time.

The Johnsons' more recent work in social interdependence theory and *cooperative controversy* with Karl Smith (Johnson et al., 2000a, 2007), added to the research. Johnson, Johnson and Smith advocated that cooperative controversy encouraged students to provide a more reasoned judgement on an issue due to the requirements of bringing together the different information, perceptions, opinions and reasoning processes leading to greater mastery and retention of material. They argued that students in competitive and individualistic situations did not have this opportunity to bring together information and reason with others.

Work in the UK on group work continued in the 1990s with a focus on how group work could help to develop a collaborative approach (Galton and Williamson, 1992). Later work from Blatchford et al. (2003) in the UK found that group work led to positive motivation and attitudes to learning and relationships. In Australia, work from Robyn Gillies (Gillies, 2003b, 2004) and Gillies and Boyle (2006) centred around how teacher's discourse helped to promote the interaction between students, thus linking with the work of Johnson and Johnson (2000) and Johnson et al. (2007). The study by Gillies and Boyle (2006), which involved 30 primary school teachers and over 800 students who were trained in using communication skills as well as utilising cooperative learning, found that the students asked more questions and engaged in more mediated learning strategies. Gillies and Boyle (2006) analysed transcripts from teachers and found that by using the different mediated learning strategies, teachers helped to challenge students' thinking and understanding as well as helping them make connections to previous learning.

The benefits of cooperative learning

Research into the benefits has identified a number of outcomes as detailed below.

1. Improved academic outcomes

Extensive research evidence suggests cooperative learning is an effective strategy for maximising learning outcomes of all students (Gillies and Ashman, 2003; Johnson and Johnson, 1994; Johnson et al., 2000a; Slavin, 1995b, 1996). Gillies (1999, 2003a) and Gillies and Ashman (1996, 1998) conducted a number of field-based, intervention studies from 1996 to 2003 in Australian schools with students from grade one to grade eight, for a period of 12 weeks to nine months. They found that students in structured groups exhibited more cooperative behaviours than the others. These students also gave more unsolicited explanations, tuning in to their group members and offering help without it being requested. They also used more cognitive language strategies and their verbal interactions helped them achieve higher achievement of outcomes than the unstructured groups' students – for example, tasks requiring cooperative talk encouraged explanation as well as application of knowledge (Gillies, 2003b).

Johnson and Johnson (1994) and Slavin (1995b) argue that there is a positive correlation between academic achievement and students giving explanations. Johnson and Johnson found from 305 studies comparing cooperative, competitive and individualistic learning on individual achievements (with 82% of findings published in journals) that cooperation was more effective than competition and promoted interpersonal relationships, social support and self-esteem, as well as higher academic achievement. Slavin's field experiment research in the 1980s and 1990s found that cooperative learning with group goals and individual accountability led to greater academic achievement than traditional methods (Slavin, 1983, 1985). Students demonstrated the ability to provide explanations, instructions and develop implicit understanding of the needs of other group members in a cooperative learning situation. Cooperative learning has also been shown to promote reading and writing achievements in middle school students (Stevens, 2003) and better classroom results for special needs students (Jenkins et al., 2003). Likewise, Watson's (1999) study in a small special education class of eight students with moderate learning difficulties, found that despite them not initially relating well to each other prior to the implementation of group work, after strategies to further group work showed heightened emotional engagement as well as increased social awareness. This could explain the results of Jenkins et al.'s (2003) study, in which 21 classroom teachers who used cooperative learning were interviewed, and which found that when using cooperative learning, there was a broad range of benefits for their special needs students including increased self-esteem, provision of a safe learning environment and greater success on learning tasks.

When using cooperative learning in comparison with more teacher-centred learning approaches, teachers were more likely to ask more cognitive and meta-cognitive questions so that students are required to, 'provide reasons for their answers, connect their ideas to previous learning, and justify their conclusions' (Gillies, 2007:25). Consequently, students were more likely to be engaged in higher order thinking (King et al., 1998) and pose questions to challenge others' perspectives (Palinscar and Herrenkohl, 2002). Some have argued that there are increased benefits for higher ability students who, by providing high quality explanations, develop their learning with cognitive reorganisation while giving elaborated responses and providing explanations when cooperating in learning activities (Terwel et al., 2001). However, low achieving students need opportunities too for higher-order thinking activities in order to help them use their minds well (Newmann and Wehlage, 1993) and in a cooperative learning classroom all students are involved in higher-order thinking activities. A classroom environment built by teachers who have developed their pedagogical practices to encourage cooperative work habits develops students' motivation to participate more in class activities (Morcom and Cumming-Potvin, 2010; Turner and Patrick, 2004). Cooperative learning has been shown to improve both academic and social and emotional learning outcomes for all students.

2. Social and emotional learning

Cooperative learning improves social skill development (Johnson et al., 1990; Slavin, 1995a, 1996; Stevens and Slavin, 1995b) and helps to promote socialisation and learning among students (Cohen, 1994). Cooperative learning is appropriate for younger students as they require careful and explicit teaching of the required cooperative social skills (Bruffee, 1984; 1995). It is also appropriate for older students who have not developed collaborative skills. Additionally, cooperative learning can improve social problems (Johnson et al., 2000b), alleviate bullying (Cowie and Berdondini, 2001) and help students manage conflict (Stevahn et al., 1997). Programmes such as Lipman's Philosophy for Children, which promote cooperative skills, have demonstrated that children can learn transferable skills such as critical and creative thinking and collaborative problem-solving in these situations (Trickey and Topping, 2004).

Positive social and emotional development lays the foundations for well-being and good mental health and so is an important focus for schools (Farrell and Travers, 2005; Greenberg et al., 2003). Longitudinal studies in primary schools have found that social competence has a positive correlation with academic achievement (Welsh et al., 2001; Malecki and Elliott, 2002), with Barchard's (2003) early findings also showing that there appears to be some correlation between some elements of emotional intelligence with academic outcomes, hence the need for more research in this area. Cooperative learning experiences can be used to increase students' cooperative predispositions, leading to pro-social behaviours and reducing bullying and harm intended aggression in students (Choi et al., 2011). The research into social and emotional learning (Goleman, 1995) has demonstrated the importance of competencies such as self-awareness, social awareness and relationship management for 21st century learning and provided evidence for leadership qualities being supported in collaborative environments. Some of the attributes of effective leaders also rely heavily on being able to demonstrate emotionally intelligent behaviours. Leadership attributes are:

> authentic communication, instilling trust in others, building teams, effective mentoring, developing quality relationships, motivating others, managing stress, conflict resolution, fostering positive attitudes and creative and lateral decision making.
>
> *(Hansen, 2011:10)*

With strong emotional intelligence, it is more likely that students will become better leaders and so teachers can concentrate on such leadership skills during the cooperative lessons they develop.

3. Student relationships

Cooperative learning has an impact on student relationships because in a classroom of this type students assist others with their learning and, in doing so, give and receive help.

Positive relationships have been found when students provide help with the content of the task and by giving and receiving explanations (Nattiv, 1994) – this also positively affects achievement (Webb, 1991). Interactions among students are crucial to cooperative learning and the interactions that occur in the groups help to facilitate the learning (Gillies, 2002) with positive relationships occurring as students help each other and enhance thinking. In cooperative groups, rather than in other types of groups, students are more likely to demonstrate the ability to provide explanations and instructions and develop implicit understanding of the needs of other group members. Trusting relationship building is crucial, especially when teachers want to develop students who learn to respect their peers, whose values and ideas might differ to their own (Cogan et al., 2000). Research by Gillies (2002) has shown the importance of cooperative learning for a lasting impact on student learning. Students who were trained initially in the processes and skills required for successful cooperative learning, demonstrated ongoing positive relationships with other students, with the ability to help each other and enhance thinking in future cooperative learning experiences (Gillies, 2002). Trusting relationships between students, as well as between teacher and students, in such classrooms are developed and enhanced:

> The trusting relationships that are built through cooperative strategies in . . . classrooms will develop collaborative skills that are crucial for the development of both the children's emotional, as well as academic, development.
> *(Ferguson-Patrick, 2008:17)*

Including all students in learning

One of the major spin-offs from such improved relationships in the classroom is ensuring that all students are included in learning. As the work of Elizabeth Cohen has demonstrated (Cohen, 1994; Cohen and Lotan, 2014), when teachers actively include all pupils through identifying individual strengths and giving them roles in groups, then it recognises diversity as a learning resource and changes the conditions that influence students' participation in the classroom. This equity is fundamental to an intercultural classroom. This is explored in depth in Chapter 1.

Barriers to implementing cooperative learning

In spite of the extensive benefits of working together cooperatively in classrooms, as detailed above, the actual use of this pedagogy is limited worldwide (Fernández-Lozano et al. 2012; Ruys et al. 2012; Veenman et al. 2002). Large-scale studies in England by Galton et al. in 1980 – repeated in 1999 – and by Baines et al. (2009) suggest that within the majority of primary classrooms, pupils sit *in* groups but rarely work together *as* groups.

Barriers to developing cooperative learning that help explain its lack of use are twofold. The first concerns political motives that promote more traditional approaches to teaching in a drive to improve attainment, and the second concerns a lack of sufficient understanding by teachers of cooperative learning. But even when professional development has explored cooperative learning, teachers need to reconcile this approach with their own beliefs about teaching and learning.

In England, one of the key reasons for this is a strong culture of performativity (Murray, 2012) due to the demands of 'high stakes' national testing, beginning at the age of six. This can lead teachers to focus on teaching to the tests. This is in stark contrast to some other countries, most notably Finland, where teachers' professional judgements are highly respected and no external 'high stakes' assessments are carried out on pupils until the end of their statutory schooling (Sahlberg, 2015). Coupled with what has been argued is a lack of in-depth understanding of pedagogy by teachers (Simon, 1981; Alexander 2004), England has proved unfertile ground for developing cooperative learning in spite of research projects that have demonstrated the importance of collaboration and talk for learning: the Teaching and Learning Research Programme (TLRP); (James and Pollard, 2011); and the Social Pedagogic Research into Grouping (SPRinG) project (Blatchford et al., 2005). Hennesey and Diongi (2013:63) also argue in Australia that cooperative learning is, 'not well embedded in teacher training nor traditionally supported in schools', and state that this is because, 'many educators are not well trained, often seek shortcuts to quality group work, perceive time as a barrier to its implementation, and/or tend to assume that traditional classroom groups will suffice' (Antil et al., 1998; Johnson and Johnson, 1994; as cited in Hennesey and Diongi, 2013:54).

However, one major international change is taking place: assessing 15-year-old students' collaborative problem-solving skills as part of the PISA assessments, which to date have focused on mathematics, science and reading. This has been piloted in 2015 and in 2017 the OECD will publish its first country rankings (http://www.oecd.org/edu/pisa-2015-results-volume-v-9789264285521-en.htm) and (although not in the UK) students will undertake this additional assessment. The results, which will appear in the form of international league tables alongside other results, may provide a fresh stimulus for governments to focus on skills of collaboration and problem-solving.

Implementing cooperative learning requires sustained professional development for teachers. Cooperative learning is not a 'quick fix'. Indeed, as noted in an earlier study, 'cooperative learning in the classroom requires cooperative learning in the staffroom' (Jolliffe, 2010:154). It requires a careful and sustained approach to develop it in the classroom; one where teachers work cooperatively to support each other to develop it effectively. One of the principal aims of this book is to demonstrate how this can be achieved.

Overview of the book

The book begins in Chapter 1 with exploring fundamental aspects. This includes an understanding of the theoretical basis of cooperative learning, so that teachers know why it works. The chapter also helps readers to review their own, possibly previously unexamined, beliefs about teaching and learning: looking at the role of the teacher; notions of control and authority; the nature of knowledge and knowing; and decision-making. Detailed exploration of key principles that are required for effective cooperative learning are also discussed, together with how to put these into practice in the classroom.

In Chapter 2, the book reviews how cooperative learning has been used in different contexts worldwide, including the successes and challenges experienced. This is a unique feature of the book in demonstrating that cooperative learning cannot just be adopted in different cultures, instead it needs to be *adapted* to that context. It is hoped that by providing a wealth of examples, teachers will be able to see that this is possible across cultural boundaries.

Chapter 3 sets out a detailed step-by-step programme for success, focusing on practical activities in the classroom – in particular, teaching the skills of working together cooperatively. It also explores a range of cooperative structures, or strategies, developing roles in groups and how to assess groups. Different types of cooperative activities are also explored.

Chapter 4 examines methods of professional development, including whole-school approaches, or using cooperative learning in an individual classroom. It includes discussion of mentoring, the use of lesson study and the use of action research methods and how this can all support the implementation of cooperative learning. This chapter also explores the potential of working in learning communities, both within a school and across schools in networks, and examines research studies into such approaches.

It is hoped that this combination of research-validated methods into developing cooperative learning, as well as the wealth of practical examples, will help in bridging the gap between the potential of cooperative learning and its actual use in classrooms.

(Note: throughout the book, we have referred to 'pupils' and 'children' to indicate all levels and types of learners.)

References

Abdullahi, S. A. (2011). Rethinking global education in the twenty-first century. *World Studies in Education*, (12), 77–91.

Alexander, R. (2004). Still no pedagogy? Principle, pragmatism and compliance in primary education. *Cambridge Journal of Education*, *34*, 8–33.

Ananiadou, K. & Claro, M. (2009). *21st century skills and competences for new millennium learners in OECD countries*. OECD Publishing: Paris.

Aronson, E., Blaney, N., Stephen, C., Sikes, J. & Snapp, M. (1978). *The jigsaw classroom*, Beverley Hills, CA: Sage.

Aronson, B. & Laughter, J. (2015). The theory and practice of culturally relevant education: A synthesis of research across content areas. *Review of Educational Research*, *86*, 163–206.

Baines, E., Rubie-Davies, C., & Blatchford, P. (2009). Improving pupil group work interaction and dialogue in primary classrooms: Results from a year-long intervention study. *Cambridge Journal of Education*, *39*(1), 95–117.

Barchard, K. (2003). Does emotional intelligence assist in the prediction of academic success? *Educational and Psychological Measurement*, *63*, 840–858.

Brand, B. R., & Triplett, C. F. (2012). Interdisciplinary curriculum: An abandoned concept? *Teachers and Teaching*, *18*(3), 381–393.

Britton, J. (1970). *Language and learning*. London: Allen Lane.

Brody, C. M. & N. Davidson, (Eds.), (1998). *Professional development for cooperative learning: Issues and approaches*. Albany, NY: State University of New York Press.

Bruner, J. (1996). *The culture of education*. London: Harvard University Press.

Blatchford, P., Kutnick, P., Baines, E. & Galton, M. (2003). Towards a social pedagogy of classroom group work. *International Journal of Educational Research, 39*, 153–172.

Blatchford, P., Galton, M., Kutnick, P., & Baines, E. (2005). Improving the effectiveness of pupil groups in classrooms. *Final report to ESRC (L139 25 1046)*.

Bruffee, K. (1984). Collaborative learning and the 'Conversation of mankind'. *College English*, (46), 635–653.

Bruffee, K. (1995). Sharing our toys: Cooperative learning versus collaborative learning. *Change*, 12–18.

Choi, J., Johnson, D. & Johnson, R. (2011). Relationships among cooperative learning experiences, social interdependence, children's aggression, victimization, and prosocial behaviors. *Journal of Applied Social Psychology, 41*, 976–1003.

Cogan, J. & Grossman, D. (2009). Characteristics of globally minded teachers: A twenty-first century view. In: T. Kirkwood-Tucker (Ed.), *Visions in global education: The globalization of curriculum and pedagogy in teacher education and schools*. 240–255. New York: Peter Lang.

Cogan, J., Grossman, D. & Lui, M. (2000). Citizenship: the democratic imagination in a global/ local context. *Social Education, 64*, 48–52.

Cohen, E. (1986). *Designing groupwork*. New York: Teachers College Press.

Cohen, E. (1994). Restructuring the classroom: Conditions for productive small groups. *Review of Educational Research, 64*, 1–35.

Cohen, E. G., & Lotan, R. A. (2014). *Designing groupwork: Strategies for the heterogeneous classroom*. (3rd edition). New York: Teachers College Press.

Cowie, H. & Berdondini, L. (2001). Children's reactions to cooperative group work: A strategy for enhancing peer relationships among bullies, victims and bystanders. *Learning and Instruction, 11*, 517–530.

Damon, W. & Phelps, E. (1989). Critical distinctions among three approaches to peer education. *International Journal of Educational Research, 13*, 9–19.

Deardorff, D. K. (2006). Identification and assessment of intercultural competence as a student outcome of internationalization. *Journal of Studies in International Education, 10*, 241–266.

Dillenbourg, P. (1999). What do you mean by collaborative learning? In: P. Dillenbourg, (Ed.), *Collaborative learning: Cognitive and computational approaches*. Oxford: Elsevier.

Dillenbourg, P., Baker, M., Blaye, A. & O'Malley, C. (1996). The evolution of research on collaborative learning. In: E. Spada & P. Reiman (Eds.), *Learning in humans and machine: Towards an interdisciplinary learning science*. Oxford: Elsevier.

Farrell, P. & Travers, T. (2005). A healthy start: Mental health promotion in early childhood settings. *Australian e-Journal for the Advancement of Mental Health, 4*, 1–10.

Ferguson-Patrick, K. (2008). The values of citizenship in a cooperative classroom: Early career teachers' perspectives. *The Social Educator, 26*, 11–18.

Ferguson-Patrick, K. (2014). *Establishing a democracy classroom: Cooperative learning and good teaching*. PhD: University of Newcastle.

Fernández-Lozano, M. P., González-Ballesteros, M., & De-Juanas, A. (2012). The scope of cooperative work in the classroom from the viewpoint of primary school teachers. *Journal of Research in Educational Psychology, 10*(1), 171–194.

Florian, L. & Black-Hawkins, K. (2011). Exploring inclusive pedagogy. *British Educational Research Journal, 37*, 813–828.

Fujikane, H. (2003). Approaches to global education in the United States, the United Kingdom and Japan. *Comparative education*. New York: Springer.

Galton, M. & Williamson, J. (1992). *Group work in the primary classroom*. Abingdon: Routledge.

Galton, M., Hargreaves, L., Comber, C., Wall, D. & Pell, A. (1999). *Inside the primary classroom 20 years on*. London: Routledge.

Galton, M., Simon, B. & Croll, P. (1980). *Inside the primary classroom*. London: Routledge and Kegan Paul.

Gay, G. (2000). *Culturally responsive teaching: Theory, research, and practice*. New York: Teachers College Press.

Gillies, R. M. (1999). Maintenance of cooperative and helping behaviours in reconstituted groups. *The Journal of Educational Research, 92*, 357–363.

Gillies, R. (2002). The residual effects of cooperative learning experiences: A two-year follow-up. *The Journal of Educational Research, 96*, 15–21.

Gillies, R. (2003a). The behaviors, interactions, and perceptions of junior high school students during small-group learning. *Journal of Educational Psychology, 95*, 137–147.

Gillies, R. (2003b). Structuring cooperative group work in classrooms. *International Journal of Educational Research, 39*, 35–49.

Gillies, R. M. (2004). The effects of communication training on teachers' and students' verbal behaviours during cooperative learning. *International Journal of Educational Research, 41*, 257–279.

Gillies, R. (2007). High school teachers' discourse and pedagogical practices during cooperative learning. *Australian Association for Research in Education Conference*. Freemantle, WA.

Gillies, R. M. & Ashman, A. (1996). Teaching collaborative skills to primary school children in classroom-based work groups. *Journal of Educational Psychology, 6*, 187–200.

Gillies, R. M. & Ashman, A. (1998). Behavior and interactions of children in cooperative groups in lower and middle elementary grades. *Journal of Educational Psychology, 90*, 746–757.

Gillies, R. & Ashman, A. (2003). An historical review of the use of groups to promote socialization and learning. In: R. Gillies & A. Ashman (Eds.), *Cooperative learning: The social and intellectual outcomes of learning in groups*. London: RoutledgeFalmer.

Gillies, R. & Boyle, M. (2006). Ten elementary teachers' discourse and reported pedagogical practices during cooperative learning. *The Elementary School Journal, 106*, 429–451.

Goleman, D. (1995). *Emotional intelligence*. New York: Bantom Books.

Greenberg, M., Weissberg, R., O'Brien, M., Zins, J., Fredericks, L., Resnik, H. & Al, E. (2003). Enhancing school-based prevention and youth development through coordinated social, emotional and academic learning. *American Psychologist, 58*, 466–474.

Hansen, K. (2011). Emotional intelligence in educational settings. *Education Connect*, 1–23.

James, M. & Pollard, A. (2011): TLRP's ten principles for effective pedagogy: Rationale, development, evidence, argument and impact. *Research Papers in Education, 26*(3), 275–328

Jenkins, J., Antil, L., Wayne, S. & Vadasy, P. (2003). How cooperative learning works for special education and remedial students. *Exceptional Children, 69*, 279–292.

Johnson, D. (1984). *Circles of learning: Cooperation in the classroom*. Alexandria, VA: Association for Supervision and Curriculum Development.

Johnson, D. & Johnson, R. (1975). *Learning together and alone: Cooperation, competition, and individualization*. Englewood Cliffs, NJ: Prentice-Hall.

Johnson, D. & Johnson, R. (1994). *Learning together and alone: Cooperative, competitive and individualistic learning*. Boston, MA: Allyn and Bacon.

Johnson, D. & Johnson, R. (1999). What makes cooperative learning work. In: D. Kluge, S. Mcguire, D. Johnson & R. Johnson (Eds.), *JALT applied materials: Cooperative learning.* Tokyo: Japan Association for Language Teaching.

Johnson, D. W., & Johnson, R. T. (2000). *Constructive controversy.* Oxford: Blackwell Publishing Ltd.

Johnson, D. & Johnson, R. (2005). Essential components of peace education. *Theory into Practice, 44,* 280–293.

Johnson, D., Johnson, R. & Holubec, E. (1990). *Circles of learning: Cooperation in the classroom.* Alexandria, VA: Association for Supervision and Curriculum Development.

Johnson, D., Johnson, R. & Smith, K. (2000a). Constructive controversy: The educative power of intellectual conflict. *Change, 32,* 28–38.

Johnson, D., Johnson, R. & Smith, K. (2007). The state of cooperative learning in postsecondary and professional settings. *Educational Psychology Review, 19,* 15–29.

Johnson, D., Johnson, R. & Stanne, M. (2000b). *Cooperative learning methods: A meta-analysis* [Online]. Available: www.researchgate.net/profile/David_Johnson50/publicaion/220040324_Cooperative_learning_methods_A_meta-analysis/links/00b4952b39d258145c000000/Cooperative-learning-methods-A-meta-analysis.pdf [accessed 26.11.17].

Jolliffe, W. (2010). Implementing cooperative learning in a multi-dimensional community of practice. *International Association for the Study of Cooperation in Education (IASCE).* Brisbane: University of Queensland.

Kagan, S. (1989). The structural approach to cooperative learning. *Educational leadership, 47*(4), 12–15.

Kagan, S. (1994). *Cooperative learning (2).* San Juan Capistrano, CA: Kagan Cooperative Learning.

Kelly, G. (1955) *The psychology of personal constructs.* New York: W. W. Norton.

Kereluik, K., Mishra, P., Fahnoe, C. & Terry, L. (2013). What knowledge is of most worth: Teacher knowledge for 21st century learning. *Journal of Digital Learning in Teacher Education, 29,* 127–140.

King, A., Stafferi, A. & Adelgais, A. (1998). Mutual peer tutoring: Effects of structuring tutorial interaction to scaffold peer learning. *Journal of Educational Psychology, 90,* 134–152.

Ladwig, J. (2010). Beyond academic outcomes. *Review of Research in Education, 34,* 113–141.

Lewin, K. (1946). Action research and minority problems. *Journal of Social Issues, 11,* 34–46.

Lingard, B. & Keddie, A. (2013). Redistribution, recognition and representation: Working against pedagogies of indifference. *Pedagogy, Culture and Society, 21,* 427–447.

Malecki, C. & Elliott, S. (2002). Children's social behaviours as predictors of academic achievement: A longitudinal analysis. *School Psychology Quarterly, 17,* 1–23.

Merryfield, M. (1998). Pedagogy for global perspectives in education: Studies of teachers' thinking and practice. *Theory and Research in Social Education, 26,* 342–379.

Mills, M. & Gale, T. (2010). *Schooling in disadvantaged communities.* New York: Springer.

Morcom, V. & Cumming-Potvin, W. (2010). Bullies and victims in a primary classroom: Scaffolding a collaborative community of practice. *Issues in Educational Research, 20*(2).

Morrison, K. A., Robbins, H. H. & Rose, D. G. (2008). Operationalizing culturally relevant pedagogy: A synthesis of classroom-based research. *Equity and Excellence in Education, 4,* 433–452.

Murray, J. (2012). Performativity cultures and their effects on teacher educators' work. *Research in Teacher Education, 2*(2) 19–23.

Nattiv, A. (1994). Helping behaviors and math achievement gain of students using cooperative learning. *The Elementary School Journal, 94,* 285–297.

Newmann, F. & Wehlage, G. (1993). Five standards of authentic instruction. *Educational Leadership, 50,* 1–7.

NSW Department of Education (2016). *Racism no way.* NSW Government.

Palinscar, A. & Herrenkohl, L. (2002). Designing collaborative contexts. *Theory into Practice, 41,* 26–35.

Perry, L. & Southwell, L. (2011). Developing intercultural understanding and skills: Models and approaches. *Intercultural Education, 22,* 453–466.

Portera, A. (2008). Intercultural education in Europe: Epistemological and semantic aspects. *Intercultural education, 19,* 481–491.

Portera, A. and Grant C. A. (Eds.), (2017). *Intercultural education and competences: Challenges and answers for the globalised world.* Newcastle upon Tyne: Cambridge Scholars.

Rorty, R. (1979). *Philosophy and the mirror of nature.* Princeton, NJ: Princeton University Press.

Ruys, I., Keer, H. V., & Aelterman, A. (2012). Examining pre-service teacher competence in lesson planning pertaining to collaborative learning. *Journal of Curriculum Studies, 44*(3), 349–379.

Sahlberg, P. (2015). *Finnish lessons 2.0.* (2nd edn). New York: Teachers College.

Schmuck, R. A. & Schmuck, P. A. (2001) *Group processes in the classroom.* (8th edn). Boston, MA: McGraw Hill.

Schul, J. (2011). Revisiting an old friend: The practice and promise of cooperative learning for the twenty-first century. *The Social Studies, 102,* 88–93.

Sharan, S. (1990) *Cooperative learning: Theory and research.* Westport, CN: Praeger.

Sharan, Y. & Sharan, S. (1976). *Small group teaching.* Englewood Cliffs, NJ: Educational Technology Publications.

Shear, L., Novais, G., Means, B., Gallagher, L. & Langworthy, M. (2010). *ITL research design.* Menlo Park, CA: SRI International. www.sri.com/work/publications/itl-research-design [accessed 26.11.17]

Simon, B. (1981). Why no pedagogy in England? In: B. Simon & W. Taylor (Eds.), *Education in the eighties: The central issues.* London: Batsford.

Slavin, R. (1995a). The cooperative elementary school: Effects on students' achievement, attitudes, and social relations. *American Educational Research Journal, 32,* 321–351.

Slavin, R. (1995b). *Cooperative learning: Theory, research, and practice.* Boston, MA: Allyn and Bacon.

Slavin, R. (1996). *Education for all.* Exton, PA: Swets & Zeitlinger.

Slavin, R. E. (1983). When does cooperative learning increase student achievement? *Psychological bulletin, 94,* 429.

Slavin, R. E. (1985). *An introduction to cooperative learning research: Learning to cooperate, cooperating to learn.* New York: Springer.

Slavin, R. (1987). Cooperative learning: Where behavioural and humanistic approaches to classroom motivation meet. *The Elementary School Journal, 88,* 29–37.

Smith, B. & MacGregor, J. (1992). What is collaborative learning? In: A. Goodsell, M. Mayer, V. Tinto, B. Smith & J. MacGregor (Eds.), *Collaborative learning: A sourcebook for higher education.* Pennsylvania: National Centre for Postsecondary Teaching and Learning, and Assessment at Pennsylvania State University.

Starkey, H. (2012). Human rights, cosmopolitanism and utopias: Implications for citizenship education. *Cambridge Journal of Education, 42,* 21–35.

Stevahn, L., Johnson, D., Johnson, R., Green, K. & Laginski, A. (1997). Effects on high school students on conflict resolution training integrated into English literature. *Journal of Social Psychology, 137,* 302–315.

Stevens, R. (2003). Student team reading and writing: A cooperative learning approach to middle school literacy instruction. *Educational Research and Evaluation, 9,* 137–160.

Stevens, R. & Slavin, R. (1995). Effects of a cooperative learning approach in reading and writing on academically handicapped and non-handicapped students. *The Elementary School Journal, 95*, 241–263.

Terwel, J., Gillies, R., Van Den Eden, P. & Hoek, D. (2001). Cooperative learning processes of students: A longitudinal multilevel perspective. *British Journal of Educational Psychology, 71*, 619–645.

Trickey, S. & Topping, K. (2004). 'Philosophy for Children': A systematic review. *Research Papers in Education, 19*, 365–380.

Turner, J. & Patrick, H. (2004). Motivational influences on student participation in classroom learning opportunities. *Teachers College Record, 16*, 1750–1785.

United Nations Economic Scientific and Cultural Organization [UNESCO] (2013). *Intercultural competences: Conceptual and operational framework.* Paris: UNESCO.

UNESCO (2006). *Guidelines on intercultural education.* Paris: UNESCO.

Veenman, S., van Benthum, N., Bootsma, D., van Dieren, J., & van der Kemp, N. (2002). Cooperative learning and teacher education. *Teaching and Teacher Education, 18*(1), 87–103.

Vygotsky, L. (1978). *Mind in society: The development of higher psychological processes.* Cambridge, MA: Harvard University Press.

Watson, J. (1999). Working in groups: Social and cognitive effects in a special class. *British Journal of Special Education, 26*, 87–95.

Webb, N. M. (1991). Task-related verbal interaction and mathematics learning in small groups. *Journal for Research in Mathematics Education, 22*, 366–389.

Welsh, M., Parke, R., Widamen, K. & O'Neill, R. (2001). Linkages between children's social and academic competence: A longitudinal analysis. *Journal of School Psychology, 39*, 463–481.

Williams, P. & Sheridan, S. (2006). Collaboration as one aspect of quality: A perspective of collaboration and pedagogical quality in educational settings. *Scandinavian Journal of Educational Research, 50*, 83–93.

Zhao, Y. (2010). Preparing globally competent teachers: A new imperative for teacher education. *Journal of Teacher Education, 61*, 422–431.

1
UNDERSTANDING THEORY AND PRINCIPLES

Learning objectives for this chapter

By reading this chapter you will develop your understanding of the following:

- the importance of examining beliefs about learning and how they influence practice;
- contrasting perspectives about learning and teaching;
- theoretical perspectives that help explain why cooperative learning is effective;
- key principles that are required for effective cooperative learning;
- the impact of cooperative learning on inclusion to promote democratic classrooms.

Introduction

This chapter begins by exploring beliefs about teaching and learning before looking in depth at the theoretical underpinnings that help explain why cooperative learning is a powerful pedagogy and, when well implemented, it engages, motivates and supports learners. Examining the key elements that are essential to ensure genuine cooperative learning, and how to put these into practice, are discussed in depth. The chapter also demonstrates how cooperative learning supports inclusion to create a democratic intercultural classroom.

Conceptions about learning

Our philosophy, beliefs and values inform our practice and as Brody (1998:25) argues:

> Teachers' beliefs may have the greatest impact on what teachers do in the classroom, the ways they conceptualize their instruction, and learn from experience.

Beliefs are unlikely to be explicit, but identifying these is an important first step before considering new perspectives. Without reconciling our beliefs or preconceptions, we are unlikely to successfully implement or sustain a new approach to teaching. One useful starting point is to consider the differences using metaphors to explore what it means to be a teacher.

ACTIVITY: METAPHORS FOR BEING A TEACHER

Consider the following metaphors that help describe the work of teachers and, if possible, discuss the differences that each imply with colleagues:

Teachers are:

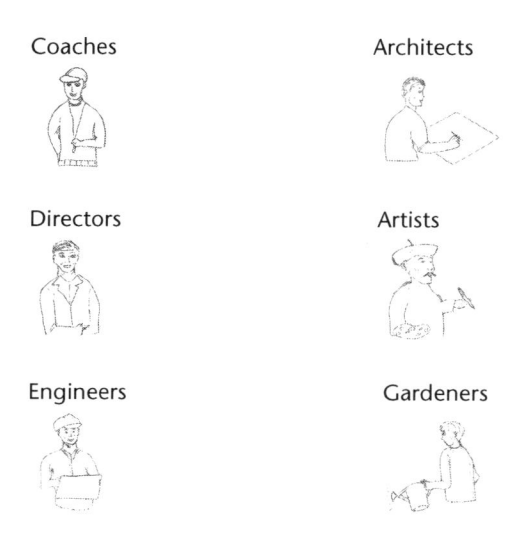

Coaches

Architects

Directors

Artists

Engineers

Gardeners

Examining teachers' beliefs

These metaphors exemplify very different conceptions about the role of the teacher. These are centred on beliefs about such aspects as: control and authority in teaching; the nature of knowledge and knowing; and the teacher's role in decision-making. These have a fundamental impact on practice and are important concepts to examine when considering the use of cooperative learning. In exploring different approaches to teaching, three broad orientations have evolved from the work of Miller and Seller (1985):

1. The transmission approach
    This approach views the aim of education as the transmission of knowledge to pupils. The teacher usually initiates this through a form of exposition

and pupils respond in a structured learning situation, usually carrying out tasks to reinforce what has been taught. In this approach, teachers have a directive role in the learning and determine how the lesson is structured. There is often an emphasis on external rewards and usually little focus on individual differences.

2. The transactional approach

    This approach sees education as a dialogue between the student and the curriculum with the student as a problem-solver. Learning can occur in a number of ways and the teacher is seen as a facilitator who provides the environment for learning. In this approach, social skills are as important as intellectual skills, due to the role of talk to support learning. Pupils share control of the learning as they carry out tasks and each student's level of development is considered. Motivation is generally intrinsic as the learner is driven by the need to solve problems and carry out tasks.

3. The transformational approach

    In this approach, the aims of education are social change and personal fulfilment. Learning focuses on the physical, cognitive, affective and spiritual/moral dimensions and the teacher's role is to link skills with these to aspects. Pupils have maximum control over their learning so they become self-motivated. Multiple perspectives are promoted and are explored through collaboration and dialogue. The focus is on participatory communities and classroom democracy and social justice is a goal.

Watkins (2005) argues that, *the development of learning communities should be a key feature of twenty-first century schools* (2005:58). He further explores what 'a learning community' means and proposes an ABCD model:

> Community as a collective, in which each member is an
> Active participant, a sense of
> Belonging has developed,
> Collaboration between members of the community is frequent, and
> Diversity of members is celebrated.
>
> *(Watkins, 2005:21)*

However, Watkins (2005:8) argues the dominant image of learning, which has become 'locked in' over centuries, is the transmission approach in which learning equates to being taught.

Now consider your own beliefs and turn to the questionnaire on page 40 which highlights key differences in these approaches and provides a useful starting point for reflection and discussion. You will also find some suggested answers. Cooperative learning spans both the transactional and the transformational approaches as the following section on theoretical perspectives explains further.

Theoretical perspectives

Research clearly shows us that one of the first steps in implementing cooperative learning is for teachers to have a clear understanding of why it works (Brody and Davidson 1998; Johnson and Johnson 1989; Sharan, 2010). This chapter aims to provide an explanation of the theories that underpin cooperative learning and to demonstrate, as stated by Lewin (1951:169), 'there is nothing as practical as a good theory'.

Cooperative learning has evolved from several theoretical perspectives. Slavin (2015) cites four major ones: motivational; cognitive developmental; cognitive elaboration; and perhaps the most developed theory, social cohesion, or social interdependence. Each of these will be explored in depth before considering how such differing perspectives can contribute to our understanding of cooperative learning.

Motivational perspective

The motivational perspective focuses on the importance of motivation in learning. When cooperative learning is structured in such a way that individuals can only complete a task and achieve their personal goals through the success of the group in which they are working, they must ensure they help others in the group to succeed. This perspective focuses on a strong sense of belonging or 'team spirit' being established and, just as is the way in sport, there is a strong desire to support the team. This is often reinforced through team rewards for the efforts of the group. But Slavin (1995, 2015) maintains that the normal classroom ethos is one of competition where individuals succeed at the cost of others. In this context, when pupils are perceived as working hard, they are often described by their peers as 'teacher's pets'. However, when they work together in teams, they strive for a common goal and are motivated to try hard and help each other. It is for this reason that group incentives that reward their joint efforts are built into many approaches to cooperative learning. David and Roger Johnson, who are among the pioneers of cooperative learning, in some cases give pupils grades based on group performance (Johnson et al., 1998). The rationale is that if pupils value the success of the group, they will encourage and help one another to achieve. Slavin's approach often includes certificates or other recognition if their average team scores on quizzes or individual assignments exceed a pre-established criterion (1994, 1995). In Student Teams–Achievement Divisions (STAD) (Slavin, 1994), children work in mixed-ability teams to master material initially presented by the teacher and then take individual tests. The teams may earn certificates based on the degree to which team members have improved their own performance from previous tests.

Slavin (1995) cites studies that have examined the impact of such approaches. Of 32 elementary studies of cooperative learning methods that provided group rewards based on the sum of group members' individual learning, 28 of them (88%) found positive effects on achievement.

KEY LEARNING POINTS: MOTIVATIONAL PERSPECTIVE

- When pupils value the success of the group, they will encourage and help one another to succeed.
- Group rewards help motivate teams and support the effectiveness of cooperative learning.
- Group rewards should be based on the individual effort and learning of all group members.

Cognitive perspectives

Cognitive perspectives hold that interactions among pupils will support learning as they support the mental processing of information or concepts. That is, through interacting, discussing and explaining, they are processing and clarifying their thinking. The reason for the success of working cooperatively is therefore not centred on motivation, but rather focuses on the cognitive processes that this stimulates. This perspective has two strands: first, cognitive developmental, which is largely derived from the work of Piaget (1926) and Vygotsky (1978); and second, cognitive elaboration (Callender and McDaniel 2009; Schunk 2012; Topping 1996; Topping et al., 2016). The following section explores these strands further.

Cognitive developmental perspective

This perspective is based on the premise that interaction among children on tasks increases their mastery of concepts. Piaget's theory (Piaget, 1926; Piaget and Inhelder, 1969) helps in understanding that peer interaction is important in questioning, or as Piaget terms it, 'creating a state of disequilibrium within a child's own perceptions'. Through this cognitive conflict, a child is stimulated to revise their own thinking, improve understanding and thereby enhance cognitive development. Johnson and Johnson (1979) have developed this as controversy theory, which argues that when someone is confronted with opposing points of view, it creates uncertainty resulting in a process of reconceptualisation and a more thoughtful conclusion. Vygotsky (1978) claimed that our mental functions are inextricably linked to our social relationships. He believed in the importance of the more knowledgeable other, who can guide learning through the concept he developed of the zone of proximal development, which is:

> the distance between the actual development level (of the child) as determined through problem solving and the level of potential development as determined through problem solving under adult guidance or in collaboration with more capable peers.

(Vygotsky, 1978:86)

He also emphasises the central importance of language as a means of communicating with others, including 'inner speech' which is the process when language and thought unite to create verbal thinking and which enables, 'thinking in pure meanings' (Vygotsky 1962:149). Thus, for both Piaget and Vygotsky, interaction between pupils is the key to learning. Slavin's (1995) research found that the cognitive processes described by developmental theorists are mediating variables that help explain the positive outcomes of cooperative learning.

Cognitive elaboration perspective

The cognitive elaboration perspective focuses on the importance of some kind of cognitive restructuring, or elaboration if the learner is to retain what is being learned and relate it to other already known concepts (Callender and McDaniel, 2009; Schunk 2012). One of the most effective methods of doing this is to explain or teach the information to someone else. This process is at the heart of many cooperative activities. Research into peer tutoring (Topping 1996; Topping et al., 2016) in which two pupils work together – one providing the other with assistance in actively acquiring knowledge and skills – has found achievement benefits for the tutor as well as the tutee in working in this way. This aligns with the theory that we consolidate and extend our learning by teaching it to someone else. Studies have shown that pupils working together on activities can learn material far better than through working alone (O'Donnell, 2006). Studies of the impact of reciprocal teaching (Webb, 2008; Palincsar et al., 1987; Sporer et al., 2009) have supported the positive effects on student achievement.

KEY LEARNING POINTS: COGNITIVE PERSPECTIVES

- Through interacting, discussing and explaining, pupils are processing and clarifying their thinking.
- Peer interaction is important in questioning a child's previously held conceptions and developing these further.
- In order to retain information in the memory and relate it to what is already known, some form of restructuring or elaboration is necessary.
- One of the most effective means of elaboration is explaining, or teaching, to someone else.

Social cohesion perspectives

The social cohesion perspective holds that the effects of cooperative learning on achievement are mediated by the cohesiveness of the group. In summary, pupils will engage in tasks and help one another because they identify with the group and want it to succeed. In this perspective, one of the key elements is the need for team-building to ensure the cohesion of the group prior to carrying out tasks. These theorists do not see group rewards as important, as the intrinsic sense of reward, achieved through the satisfaction in the group's success, is more important than achieving extrinsic rewards and can introduce an element of competition (Johnson and Johnson, 1989). They emphasise that the effects of cooperative learning on pupils and on pupil achievement depend substantially on the quality of the group's interaction (Battisch et al., 1993). This quality of interaction is explained through the interdependence between pupils and has led to the development of social interdependence theory.

Social interdependence theory

The roots of social interdependence theory are in the gestalt school of psychology, dating back to the early 1900s and the work of Dewey who believed that school should prepare children for participating in a democratic society. His work led to the early development of inquiry in small groups based on pupils' interests. Lewin (1948) laid the foundations for the group dynamics movement which focused on creating effective relationships in groups. This was further developed by Deutsch (1949, 1962) who studied cooperation and conflict and conceptualised one of the principles of cooperative learning: positive interdependence in which each student in a group is responsible for contributing to the learning of others. Social interdependence was further developed by the work of social psychologists, such as Johnson and Johnson (1975), Johnson and Holubec (1990), Schmuck and Schmuck (2001), and Sharan (1990). Social interdependence theory proposes that there are two types of interdependence: positive and negative (Johnson and Johnson, 1989). Positive interdependence exists when individuals realise they can only reach their goals if others with whom they are positively linked achieve theirs. In contrast, negative interdependence is where individuals can only reach their goals if others fail to reach theirs. Positive interdependence results in mutual help and assistance, whereas negative interdependence would lead to obstructing others. Positive interdependence leads to promotive interaction as individuals encourage each other's efforts to learn. This results in increased efforts to achieve, positive interpersonal relationships and psychological health (Johnson and Johnson, 1989, 2008).

Different approaches to cooperative learning developed by Elizabeth Cohen (1994), Shloma and Yael Sharan's group investigation (1992) and Aronson's jigsaw method (Aronson et al., 1978) make use of individual roles in groups to carry out key aspects. This helps create interdependence among the group, and this 'positive interdependence' (Johnson and Johnson, 2008, 2016) is a vital element in developing genuine cooperative learning. Research by Battisch, et al. (1993),

Johnson and Johnson (2008) and Webb (2008) demonstrates that the achievement effects of cooperative learning depend on social cohesion and the quality of group interactions.

KEY LEARNING POINTS: SOCIAL COHESION PERSPECTIVES

- The achievement effects of cooperative learning depend on the social cohesion and the quality of the group interactions.
- A key aspect of this perspective is an emphasis on team-building in preparing for cooperative group work.
- Pupils will engage in the task and help one another learn because they identify with the group and want each other to succeed. This is positive interdependence.
- As long as the task is challenging and interesting and the pupils are prepared for skills in group work, they will find the experience of working together highly rewarding.

Reconciling the different perspectives

Each of the preceding theories provides an explanation of why working cooperatively is effective. Slavin (2015) proposes that these theories are not contradictory, but instead are complementary. Group goals and a sense of loyalty to a team, which are crucial to the motivational perspective, also support the social cohesion of the group. The interaction of the group provides fertile ground for questioning, developing and elaborating on ideas and concepts through teaching each other, which is the focus of cognitive perspectives. As seen in Figure 1.1, Slavin shows how these combined theories demonstrate that cooperative learning is a vehicle for enhanced learning.

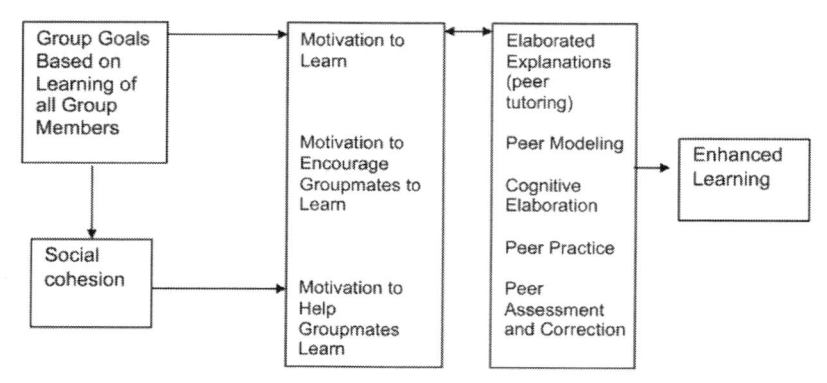

FIGURE 1.1   Slavin (2015) shows how combined theories demonstrate that cooperative learning is a vehicle for enhanced learning

Source: slavin, r. E. (2015): Cooperative learning in elementary schools, Education 3–13: *International Journal of Primary, Elementary and Early Years Education.* p.3

ACTIVITY 1.1: CHECKING YOUR UNDERSTANDING

Now read the following statements related to the major theoretical perspectives, which help explain the effectiveness of cooperative learning, and match each statement to the corresponding theory.

Statement	Theory
	1. Motivational
	2. Cognitive developmental
	3. Cognitive elaboration
	4. Social interdependence

a) Pupils help their team mates to learn because they care about the group.

b) Group rewards are built into group work including certificates or group grades.

c) Pupils learn better when they have had the opportunity to restructure or elaborate through explaining to others.

d) Collaborative activity promotes growth because children of similar ages are likely to be operating within one another's proximal zone of development.

e) The effect of cooperative learning on student achievement depends largely on the quality of the group's interaction.

f) Pupils help their team mates to learn because it is in their own interests to do so.

g) When individuals cooperate, social cognitive conflict occurs that creates cognitive disequilibrium which in turn stimulates reconceptualisation.

h) Pupils who gain the most from cooperative activities are those who provide explanations to others.

The role of talk in learning

A social cohesion perspective that explains the effectiveness of cooperative learning has talk as a central element. A number of researchers have demonstrated that talk is a vital ingredient in effective learning (Alexander 2008; Mercer, 2008; King 2008; Gillies, 2016). However, as Gillies (2016:32) states:

> Talk that challenges students' thinking and understanding will not emerge unless students are explicitly taught how to exchange ideas, provide explanations and

justifications, engage in speculative thinking, make inferences, and draw conclusions, characteristics of high-level discourse that are known to promote cognitive growth.

As Galton et al. (1999) found in two studies, repeated some 20 years apart, an increased propensity for teachers to give directions and impart facts was seen in the later study, which represented over 80% of teachers' talk in classrooms. Howe and Abedin (2013) also noted, in studying classroom dialogue over four decades, that classroom talk continued to be dominated by teachers. To avoid this, Alexander (2008) argues that teachers need to develop a pedagogical repertoire of strategies for promoting teaching and learning talk. He refers to this as **dialogic teaching**, which consists of the following five elements:

1. It is collective: children work together on tasks, as a group or class.
2. It is reciprocal: teachers and children listen to each other and comment/share ideas.
3. It is supportive: children are supported to discuss their views freely.
4. It is cumulative: teachers and children build on each other's ideas to create coherent lines of thinking.
5. It is purposeful: teachers plan and steer classroom talk with specific purposes.

Alexander argues that when teachers genuinely engage in dialogic teaching, there is more discussion in the classroom as well as talk about talk; setting ground rules for how discussions should proceed. Gillies (2004) found that when teachers are trained to use specific dialogic skills that probed and clarified pupils' thinking and encouraged talk, the results, compared with untrained classes, led to significantly higher learning outcomes.

So in spite of research that demonstrates the effectiveness of talk and collaboration in the classroom (the Educational Endowment Foundation found the impact of collaborative learning approaches on attainment to be equivalent to an additional five months of schooling – see https://educationendowmentfoundation.org.uk/resources/teaching-learning-toolkit/collaborative-learning/#effectiveness), there is limited evidence of its use and a clear need to develop teachers' knowledge and understanding of such approaches. To ensure genuine cooperative learning, it is first important to fully comprehend the key principles that make this effective and distinguish it from group work. The next section examines these principles in depth.

Principles of cooperative learning

Johnson and Johnson (1989) have distilled the essential elements that support cooperative learning. These consist of the following five aspects, which are sometimes known by the acronym 'PIGSF', or the expression, 'pigs fly!'

Positive Interdependence
Individual Accountability
Group Processing
Small Group and Interpersonal Skills
Face-to-Face Promotive Interaction

Johnson and Johnson (1989, 2014) and other researchers in the field (Kagan 1994; Cohen 1994; Slavin 1995; Sharan 2010) have identified that the most important of these elements is positive interdependence. Sharan (2010:303) who notes within the 'rich variety of methods' that evolved in using cooperative learning, that, 'positive interdependence is the one constant principle, or rule, that serves as an anchor for the design of all methods' (Sharan, 2010:308). The next section explores positive interdependence in depth.

Positive interdependence

All for one and one for all, united we stand and divided we fall.
(Alexandre Dumas, The Three Musketeers*)*

Positive interdependence exists when members of a group are linked in such a way that they cannot succeed unless everyone does. Therefore, they must work together and ensure that everyone in the group completes their goal. Through positive interdependence, group members realise that they have two responsibilities: first to learn the assigned material/task, and second, to ensure that all the group members learn it also. Johnson and Johnson (1999) note that there are two broad types of positive interdependence: **outcomes interdependence** which exists when pupils strive to achieve a goal or reward for their efforts, and **means interdependence** when pupils need to share resources, carry out different roles in groups or complete tasks to achieve the group's goals. Now examine Activity 1.2 and consider how positive interdependence can be built into lessons. This will vary according to the age of the pupils and the specific requirements of a lesson. It is important to realise that without positive interdependence, cooperation does not exist.

ACTIVITY 1.2: STEPS TO SUPPORT POSITIVE INTERDEPENDENCE

1. Ensure each group has a clearly understood task, which includes defined success criteria.
2. Structure goal interdependence so that group members believe they can only achieve it if the entire group does, for example, through providing tasks that can only be completed together.
3. Provide identity interdependence where the group develops a mutually agreed identity, such as a team name, motto, flag or symbol to support cohesion.
4. Get team members to work in pairs to carry out specific tasks or clarify their understanding, such as interviewing each other to find out specific information, or carrying out paired reading where one child reads a page or paragraph and the other then summarises what has been read, with the children swapping roles.
5. Structure resource interdependence by giving each member of the group only a portion of the information, materials or other necessary items so that group members have to combine their resources to achieve their goals (known as resource interdependence).
6. Portioning a task with children researching different aspects and becoming experts, who then have to share their knowledge with the group to put the parts of the 'jigsaw' together into a whole. This is known as the jigsaw method (Aronson et al., 1978).
7. Develop role interdependence where each member of the group is given complementary roles (such as reader, recorder, checker, resource manager, reporter, encourager, etc.).
8. Provide group rewards. This can be via giving a group score, where pupils are tested individually then combine their scores, or reward all members when a goal has been reached. This could be bonus points for the team (never to an individual), a team certificate or extra free time, etc.
9. Encourage groups to celebrate their success: this could be through a group cheer, rap, or song to emphasise the group's efforts.

Individual accountability

> What a child can do in collaboration today, he will be able to do alone tomorrow.
> *(Vygotsky, 1934/1987:211)*

Individual accountability means that each member of the group must learn to be responsible for their own contribution, otherwise the group will not succeed. This also supports one of the aims of cooperative learning, which is not just to teach pupils to work together in a group, but also to give pupils the skills to work independently. In other words, as Vygotsky says, what they can do with the help of others today, they may learn to do on their own tomorrow.

The teacher needs to structure activities to ensure that each student is participating and monitor the groups to ensure that 'everyone is contributing'; praising and rewarding groups where this is the case.

Now examine Activity 1.3 and consider how positive interdependence can be built into lessons. You will find further information about a range of cooperative structures in Appendix 1.

ACTIVITY 1.3: WAYS TO HELP ENSURE INDIVIDUAL ACCOUNTABILITY

1. Provide a safe environment where pupils feel able to respond in groups or with the whole class, without fear of ridicule, i.e. no 'put downs'! This is the fundamental part of the classroom ethos necessary for cooperative learning to thrive.
2. Keep the group sizes small, as the smaller the group the greater the sense of individual accountability.
3. Random reporting to the class of the groups' contributions, through the use of a cooperative structure such as 'numbered heads'. Here, members of a group are given a number and the teacher calls out a number when groups are ready to report – that person then has to speak for the group. Groups are not aware of which number will be called and therefore have to be sure that everyone is ready to respond.
4. Ask group members to explain their group's work to a member of another group. This can be done by the use of a cooperative structure such as 'two stay and two stray'.
5. Use of peer assessment where groups develop assessment criteria which focuses on the contribution of all members.
6. When assigning roles to groups, one pupil is given the role of checker, and checks that everyone is contributing.
7. Use group marks where the individual scores are aggregated to provide a group mark and these group marks are made public. This can instil a sense of personal responsibility to do well to support the group score.

Group processing

> Coming together is a beginning. Keeping together is progress. Working together is success.
>
> *(Henry Ford)*

One of the ways in which cooperative learning is distinguished from group work is the attention given to the social interactions of the group – not just the academic objective. Group processing can be defined as reflecting on the effectiveness of the group in a particular lesson in order to decide what worked well, and in what ways getting along together to achieve a goal can be improved. Groups need to learn to analyse their own progress and their ability to function as a group. This is a developmental process and can enable control over the quality of the work produced. This reflection can accompany other assessment for learning strategies where pupils are involved in peer- and self-assessment.

Now examine the steps in Activity 1.4 and consider the different ways to support group processing.

ACTIVITY 1.4: WAYS TO SUPPORT GROUP PROCESSING

1. Have a particular teamwork skill (such as everyone participating) which is being focused on that lesson, or for a series of lessons, and remind groups of this at the start of each lesson. During the lesson, provide praise and reinforcement to encourage the development of the skill. At the end of the lesson ask groups to evaluate their progress with the specified skill.
2. Ask pupils to set goals for themselves and their teams.
3. Ensure that time is provided for reflection – not just at the end of the lesson, but also at other key points.
4. Share teacher observations of the team interactions with the groups to support reflection.
5. Ask groups to occasionally produce short evaluations of their teamwork. You will find some examples of how to do this on the Assessing Cooperative Learning website by *Journey to Excellence*: http://circle. adventist.org/files/CD2008/CD2/j2e/practice/assessment/cooperative/ team.html.

Small group and interpersonal skills

> You can't stay in your part of the forest waiting for others to come to you. You have to go to them sometimes.
>
> *(A. A. Milne,* Winnie-the-Pooh*)*

One of the keys to success is to ensure that small group and interpersonal skills are explicitly taught; simply placing children together and expecting them to cooperate is unlikely to succeed.

Developing these skills will require an ongoing programme to teach and practise them. It is important to understand that some are more complex than others. Jolliffe (2007) produced a hierarchy of skills in the form of a four-stage rocket (see Figure 1.2). Chapter 3 explores teaching the skills in depth – however,

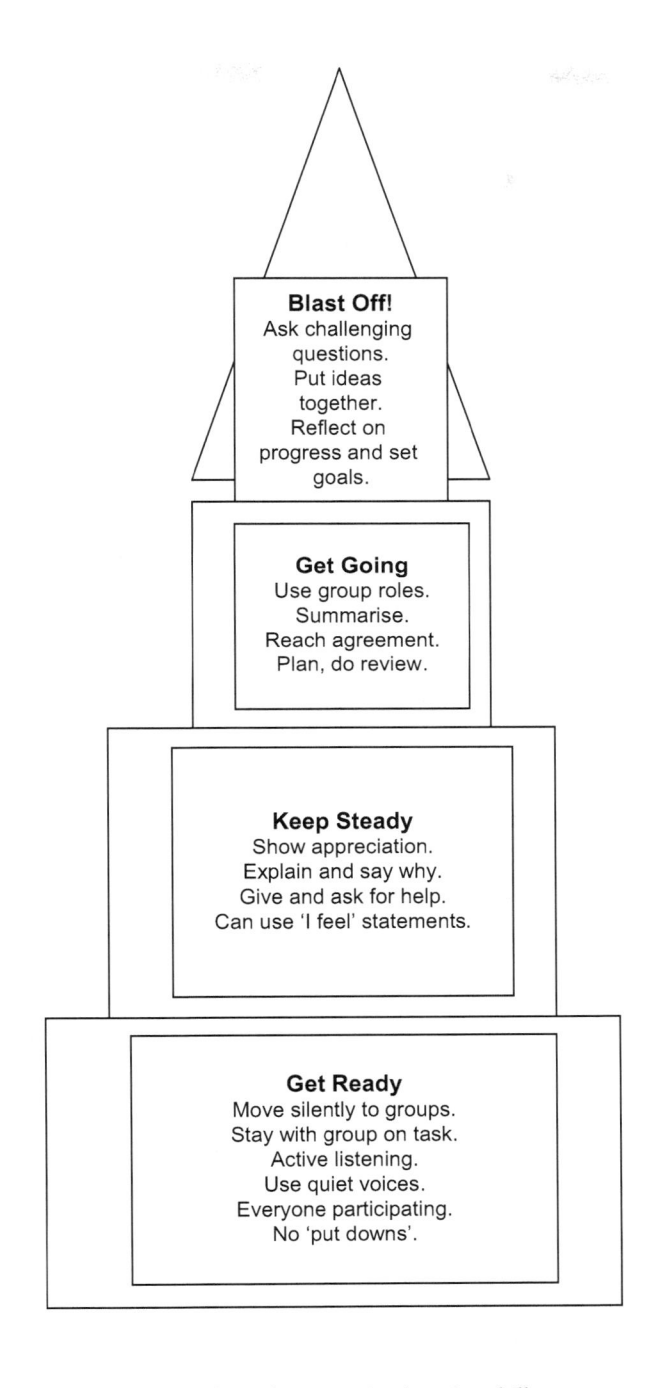

FIGURE 1.2 The four-stage rocket of cooperative learning skills

Source: Jolliffe, W. (2007) *Cooperative learning in the classroom: Putting it into practice*. London: Sage.

it is useful to note that the following are important skills to support student interaction, as noted by Gillies (2007):

Interpersonal skills

- Active listening.
- Freely stating ideas.
- Accepting responsibility for one's behaviour.
- Providing constructive criticism.

Small-group skills

- Taking turns.
- Sharing tasks.
- Making decisions democratically.
- Trying to understand the other person's perspective.
- Clarifying differences.

Now consider the steps in Activity 1.5 to help support the development of these skills. You may want to consider teaching these as part of a Personal and Social Health programme, as well as incorporating them into lessons that include cooperative learning. The use of Circle Time in classrooms can also support these skills (see www.circle-time.co.uk/our-approach/quality-circle-time).

ACTIVITY 1.5: WAYS TO SUPPORT SMALL GROUP AND INTERPERSONAL SKILLS

1. Allocate a notice board in the classroom entitled 'Social Skill of the Week'.
2. Select a skill from the interpersonal skills listed above.
3. Introduce the skill.
4. Explain the role of the week, e.g. if it is 'staying on task' then the role might be 'Taskmaster'.
5. Choose structures that support the specific skill (see Appendix 1).
6. Model the skill to the whole class and (where needed) to a group. Reinforce the skill by monitoring and rewarding groups.
7. Reflect on the skill through providing time for groups to discuss; where appropriate, ask pupils to complete reflection forms.

Face-to-face promotive interaction

We are wired to connect.

(Goleman, 2007:12)

Promotive interaction exists when individuals encourage and facilitate each other's efforts to achieve a group's goals. By promoting each other's success, pupils build academic and social skills. This is supported by the classroom organisation and layout to ensure the physical proximity needed for effective communication, or 'eye-to-eye and knee-to-knee'. It is characterised by individuals giving each other help and exchanging resources. This supports thinking skills by more active involvement with the task and greater interaction. Oral summarising, giving and receiving explanations, and elaborating (relating what is being learned to previous learning) are important types of verbal interchanges that support promotive interaction.

Now review the steps in Activity 1.6 and consider the different ways to support face-to-face promotive interaction.

ACTIVITY 1.6: WAYS TO SUPPORT FACE-TO-FACE PROMOTIVE INTERACTION

1. Ensure that for cooperative learning activities pupils are seated in small groups (preferably groups of four, and a maximum of five) facing each other. This will usually consist of two tables with four chairs placed in pairs opposite each other.
2. Strengthen the interaction and discussion that underpins the thinking process. Structures that help include summarising or paraphrasing what a partner has said using structures such as: the paraphrase game; think/pair/square; the grid; graphic organisers. (See Appendix 1 for more information.)

Supporting inclusion for a globalised classroom

Elizabeth Cohen (1994) first recognised that inequality in a class needs to be addressed in order to make effective use of group work. This can also help to challenge inequality in society more broadly. Cohen's work was based on sociological analysis of interactions in classrooms and Expectation States theory (Berger et al., 1977), that seeks to explain how beliefs about status characteristics translate into performance expectations, which in turn shapes the behaviours of individuals in a group. In other words, this helps explain how hierarchies are created in groups due to underlying beliefs about status – so that a student who is perceived to be clever and who is confident in stating their views, would have a higher status than a student who is thought to be less intelligent, particularly if that student is reluctant to participate verbally. This can fundamentally impact on the effectiveness of work in groups and in creating a democratic ethos.

Elizabeth Cohen refers to this hierarchy as a 'status problem' which she defined as, 'an agreed-upon social ranking where everyone feels it is better to have a high rank within the status order than a low rank' (Cohen 1994:27). Status can depend on academic results, popularity among peers, or societal status such as gender, ethnicity, or socio-economic class. She developed an approach to cooperative learning called **Complex Instruction (CI)**. This recognises diversity as a learning resource and changes the conditions that influence pupils' participation in the classroom (Cohen 1994, 1998; Cohen and Lotan, 1997). CI has three main components:

1. Multi-ability curricula which are designed to support higher order thinking skills through group work and are focused on a central idea or concept, with tasks that are open-ended and expect pupils to work interdependently to solve problems.
2. It uses particular strategies such as giving roles to pupils to help them manage their own groups, with the teacher monitoring and providing feedback to support equal participation.
3. Teachers recognise and treat status problems which broadens perceptions about what it means to be smart and to convince pupils that they each have important contributions to make to a task.

Cohen's Complex Instruction (1994, 2014), as with any cooperative learning approach, has a series of steps required for introduction. These start with preparing pupils for group work and teaching cooperative behaviours. She uses a series of exercises called 'Skillbuilders', which range from sharing pieces of a jigsaw puzzle and solving it cooperatively, to giving a group a beach ball and the task of keeping the ball in the air for so many minutes, as well as many other generic exercises. She recommends all of these should be followed by discussion to provide a chance for the pupils to make connections between the cooperation required in the task and their own behaviour in the group. Cohen also recommends that group norms, or rules, are created based on discussion and understanding of why it is important, for example, to ensure equal participation. Morris (1977:63) recommends the following norms for cooperative problem-solving:

1. Say your own ideas.
2. Listen to others; give everyone a chance to talk.
3. Ask others for their ideas.
4. Give reasons for your ideas and discuss many different ideas.

In order to train groups to use such norms, Cohen recommends a challenging survival problem to solve (see http://wilderdom.com/games/descriptions/SurvivalScenarios.html for a range of survival exercises).

Following the introduction of group norms, Cohen recommends planning group work in stages. This includes using a range of cooperative structures (see Appendix 1), and carefully designing a task that is 'groupworthy' (2014:68), which she recommends should:

- be open-ended and require complex problem-solving;
- provide opportunities for multi-abilities to participate and to demonstrate competence;
- address discipline-based and intellectually suitable content.

Cohen's research (1984) found the impact of working in this way on status was strong. Cohen and Lotan (1995) presented the results of two intervention studies designed to counteract the effects of status in groups. The findings from 13 elementary schools confirmed the hypothesis that the use of status treatments increased the participation of low-status pupils and had no effect on the participation of high-status pupils. As might be expected, classrooms that used these treatments more frequently found more equal-status interaction. Cohen and Lotan (1995:118) conclude, 'In the context of a multiple ability curriculum, it is possible to produce equal-status behavior in heterogeneous classrooms as well as significant gains in achievement'.

Pescarmona's (2015) research using Cohen's status treatment approach (Complex Instruction), examined how a group of Italian primary school teachers interpreted the status problem; how they defined high and low status pupils; and how they implemented status treatment in classrooms. The teachers recognised status criteria and the goal of equity promoted by Cohen's theory, but they felt challenged by the task of implementing this when combined with their own professional experience and educational purposes and contexts. Developing multiple perceptions about pupils is complex and entails being able to recognise different intelligences and abilities, so as to give pupils the opportunity to enhance their status. As a result, the teachers tended to give a wider meaning to the status problem and carried out different strategies in their own classrooms. However, this can create a more democratic environment and, as Pescarmona (2015:37) says, 'one of the principal benefits of Cohen's legacy is that it contributes to bring the issues of equity and democratic participation back to the core of the educational debate today'. A key finding from her study, which is a core theme of this book was that:

> These teachers did not develop Cohen's status treatment as a 'ready to use' package. They interwove the new ideas with their own educational perspectives. They acted according to their own educational ideas and the cultural context in which they worked.
>
> *(Pescarmona, 2015:38)*

The work of Elizabeth Cohen, and more recent research by Pescarmona (2015), highlighted the impact of creating a more democratic and equal classroom. In order to explore more fully what is meant by a 'democracy classroom', the next section examines this concept further and outlines research into putting this into practice in Australia.

Cooperative learning and democracy classrooms

Learning about and practising cooperative learning can lead to a particular classroom ambience, known as a 'democracy stance'. There are a number of markers of what actually leads to a democracy classroom, known as the **democracy indicators**. Research with early career teachers over a seven-month period in their first, second or third year of teaching demonstrated the positive impact that professional development in actual classroom pedagogy can have on classroom practice

(Ferguson-Patrick, 2014). The intent of the research was to explore the extent of the alignment between cooperative learning occurring in classrooms and elements of the NSW Quality Teaching model (NSW Department of Education and Training, 2003) in order to explore links between professional development, cooperative learning and good teaching. An additional aspect to the research indicated that the teachers were enacting a cooperative learning classroom in different ways and, additionally, all had evidence of developing a particular classroom culture – a democracy classroom was emerging. The emergence of these indicators of democracy classrooms was a key feature of the methodology of this research study.

The data collection for this research study initially involved classroom observations as teachers had an obligation to design and teach at least one cooperative learning lesson a week. It also included collections of conversations and action plan entries from professional learning sessions about cooperative learning; reflective diary entries and interviews.

Most significantly, the research found that these classrooms, where teachers were using cooperative learning as a pedagogical practice, had a democratic 'feel' about them, or as Vinterek (2010) described, they seemed to have a 'democracy stance'. In a democracy classroom, there is more likely to be strong social support as both teachers and other pupils give supportive comments and value the contributions of all. The research results indicated that the importance given to heterogeneous grouping and the structured development of social skills associated with cooperative tasks, increased this democracy stance and inclusive social support. The study demonstrated that professional development in cooperative learning supported early career teachers in improving both academic and social aspects of their classroom pedagogy and such professional development assisted them to develop democracy classrooms. As Dewey (1933:34) commented, 'democratic social arrangements promote a better quality of human experience, one which is more widely accessible and enjoyed, than do non-democratic, and anti-democratic forms of social life'. Early career teachers, supported with their pedagogy in their early years with a democracy stance, are able to develop an engaging and participatory democracy classroom.

Stance is seen as a combination of values and the pedagogies selected by teachers and the knowledge used to employ their practice. It is about a way of thinking; about the values and attitudes that teachers have that indicate a democratic perspective. It is about teachers who believe in social justice, human rights and intercultural capacity. The teachers in democracy classrooms enact a particular **democracy stance**. Pupils in democracy classrooms can also develop a democracy stance; they can develop the attitudes and values, be open-minded, take others' perspectives as they decision-make with others. The democracy stance is crucial to building a democratic class culture.

Cooperative learning supports a democracy classroom. As an intellectual pedagogy – a pedagogy where teachers teach children how to respect and support other pupils, how to value and welcome difference and diversity, and where all pupils are applauded for having a voice – it is socially supportive and inclusive (Lingard and

Keddie, 2013; Mills and Gale, 2010). Cooperative learning is a pedagogy that requires high expectations from teachers for all their pupils, hence increasing its capacity as a socially just pedagogy. Teachers can develop an inclusive democracy classroom 'in action' through cooperative learning. There are obvious links between cooperative learning classrooms and democratic classrooms. The research study (Ferguson-Patrick, 2014) demonstrated the links between the indicators of democracy with key elements of cooperative learning, as shown in Table 1.1.

TABLE 1.1 A research study demonstrated the links between a democracy classroom and key elements of cooperative learning.

Indicators (signs of democracy) of such classrooms	Cooperative learning elements
1. Culture of communication and democratic school culture	
• Willingness to listen (Vinterek, 2010).	Individual accountability. Positive interdependence and a sense of group. Face-to-face interaction.
• Willingness to express thoughts (Vinterek, 2010).	Common goal.
• Share perspectives.	Face-to-face interaction.
• Dialogue.	Common goal.
• A classroom of many voices and ears (Vinterek, 2010).	Individual accountability. Positive interdependence.
• 'Deliberative dialogues' to promote equality, freedom and justice for all (Vinterek, 2010); to promote shared work and collective action (McCoy and Scully, 2002).	Individual accountability. Reflection. Interpersonal skills.
• Climate of trust (Finnan et al., 2003).	Common goal. Individual accountability.
• High self-esteem – affective domain (Baumeister et al., 2003; Bloom et al., 1973). Improved relationships.	Reflection. Individual accountability.
• Responsibility.	Individual accountability.
• Trust in the ability of oneself (Ekman, 2007; Vinterek, 2010).	Individual accountability.
• Risk taking.	Common goal.
• Tolerance and sense of justice (Thomas and Witenberg, 2004).	Individual accountability. Positive interdependence.
• Making choices, forming opinions (Vinterek, 2010).	
• Active engagement.	Common goal. Individual accountability.
• Respect and tolerance (Vinterek, 2010).	Positive interdependence and a sense of group.
• Recognition of equal worth.	Positive interdependence.
• Democratic sentiments – open mindedness, decision-making with others, taking others' perspectives (Nagda et al., 2003).	Common goal. Interpersonal skills.

(continued)

TABLE 1.1 *(continued)*

Indicators (signs of democracy) of such classrooms	*Cooperative learning elements*
2. Community of practice (Wenger, 1998) and rich learning community	
• Tolerance.	Social skills reflection.
• Respect.	Individual accountability.
• Concern for one another (Greene, 1993).	Positive interdependence and a sense of group. Interpersonal skills.
• Shared ways (Wenger, 1998).	Face-to-face interaction. Common goal. Positive interdependence and a sense of group.
• Shared discourse (Wenger, 1998).	Face-to-face interaction. Common goal.
• Pro-social behaviours (Morcom and Cumming-Potvin, 2010).	Social skills reflection. Interpersonal skills.
• All learners participate in classroom life (Florian and Linklater, 2010).	Individual accountability. Positive interdependence and a sense of group.
3. Inclusive practice	
• Increasing participation and decreasing exclusion (Florian and Black-Hawkins, 2011).	Individual accountability. Interpersonal skills.
• Respect and respond to human differences in ways that include learners in what is available in daily classroom life (Florian and Black-Hawkins, 2011).	Common goal. Individual accountability. Positive interdependence and a sense of group.
• High self-esteem, improved relationships (Slavin, 1987).	Face-to-face interaction.
• Trusting relationships (Ferguson-Patrick, 2008).	Positive interdependence and a sense of group. Interpersonal skills.
• Learners trusted to make good decisions about learning (Florian and Black-Hawkins, 2011).	Individual accountability.
• Opportunities for learning that will be part of a shared experience – participation in a community with equity demonstrated through unity, not 'sameness' (Florian and Linklater, 2010).	Common goal. Individual accountability. Positive interdependence.
4. Social learning	
• Positive, respectful relationships (Ryan and Patrick, 2001).	Face-to-face interaction. Individual accountability. Interpersonal skills.
• Sense of belonging (Osterman, 2000).	Positive interdependence.
• Opportunities to talk about values (Lovat and Toomey, 2007).	Positive interdependence. Interpersonal skills.
• 'Relational trust' (Bryk and Schneider, 2003).	Interpersonal skills. Positive interdependence. Individual accountability.

Source: Ferguson-Patrick, S. K. (2014). *Establishing a democracy classroom: Cooperative learning and good teaching.* (PhD Thesis, University of Newcastle). Retrieved from http://hdl.handle.net/1959.13/1058776

It was evident from the data in this study that the teachers who were able to create a cooperative learning environment developed democracy classrooms. The consideration of feelings in cooperative learning classrooms by providing high social support and a strong sense of community led to this 'democracy stance' (Vinterek, 2010). It was also developed by having a strong consideration of the affective domain in cooperative learning.

These classrooms developed strong relationships and their communities of collaboration considered values and proactive social skills, leading to high self-esteem and risk-taking in their pupils. The inclusive practices used by the teachers led to a democracy school culture and this democracy stance. Teachers tried to overcome exclusion by using inclusive practices, and by building a democracy stance teachers developed a culture of communication. The importance of dialogue in cooperative learning is crucial and these classrooms contained teachers and pupils who participated, were willing to express their thoughts, exhibited a willingness to listen and demonstrated respect and tolerance: they developed this culture of communication by having this stance. They developed a community of practice with mutual relationships, shared ways and discourses (Wenger, 1998) and with a strong belief in social learning, these teachers promoted self-esteem and developed pupils who had trust in their ability. One of the case studies in Chapter 2 highlights one teacher, Julie, who has developed this democracy classroom in an Australian context and therefore highlights the benefits of adapting a 'democracy stance'. Chapter 3 will explore in depth how this can be achieved.

Conclusion

This chapter has discussed the importance of examining teachers' beliefs about learning as a starting point in adopting a pedagogy such as cooperative learning. Developing a clear understanding of the theoretical perspectives that underpin this pedagogy is also important, together with the key elements that ensure that this approach is genuinely cooperative. As we have seen from the studies cited when applying this in the classroom, it is a fundamentally different way of working which can create challenges for the teacher. The benefits are in promoting a democracy stance – one that is ideal for supporting the intercultural classroom. As Chapter 3 will examine in depth, implementing cooperative learning in a carefully staged way is vital.

Chapter summary

You should now understand:

- the importance of examining beliefs about learning;
- contrasting perspectives about learning and teaching;
- theoretical perspectives that help explain why cooperative learning is effective;
- key principles that are required for effective cooperative learning;
- the impact of cooperative learning on inclusion to promote democratic classrooms.

Questionnaire: Examining teacher beliefs

Examine the statements below and tick which you think apply most to your beliefs. You will find suggested answers as to whether each statement relates to a belief that learning and teaching is transmission, transaction, or transformation on page 41.

---

1.   Control and authority.
1.1 The authority for learning rests primarily with the teacher, who is responsible for all aspects of the learning environment.
1.2 Authority is derived from the community of learners. The teacher is primarily concerned with supporting the community and pupils are capable of defining the conditions of learning.
1.3 Authority for learning is shared with the pupils and the goal is for them to become more intrinsically motivated in their learning.
2.   The teacher's role.
2.1 The teacher is the facilitator, encourager and orchestrator of learning.
2.2 The teacher is a co-learner and an integral part of the learning community.
2.3 The teacher is the manager and director of learning.
3.   Decision-making.
3.1 Decision-making is a prescribed process which rests with the teacher.
3.2 Decision-making is made through reflection and consultation and teachers consider a range of factors and dialogue with pupils focuses on equality and social justice.
3.3 Decision-making reflects that teaching is a complex craft and decisions are best made through reflection and consultation with pupils.
4.   The nature of knowledge and knowing.
4.1 Knowledge is dynamic, changing and constructed. Knowing is multi-dimensional and contextual. Dialogue is central to creating a community of learners. Pupils and teachers are co-learners.
4.2 Knowledge is an objective body of information transmitted from teachers to pupils.
4.3 Knowledge is dynamic and changing and knowing is in relation to the knower. Depth is valued over breadth in the curriculum.

Suggested answers to questionnaire: Examining teacher beliefs

---

1.   Control and authority.

1.1 The authority for learning rests primarily with the teacher, who is responsible for all aspects of the learning environment.

Teacher-centred (transmission)

1.2 Authority is derived from the community of learners. The teacher is primarily concerned with supporting the community and pupils are capable of defining the conditions of learning.

Constructed communities (transformation)

1.3 Authority for learning is shared with the pupils and the goal is for them to become more intrinsically motivated in their learning.

Learner-centred (transaction)

2.   The teacher's role.

2.1 The teacher is the facilitator, encourager and orchestrator of learning.

Learner-centred (transaction)

2.2 The teacher is a co-learner and an integral part of the learning community.

Constructed communities (transformation)

2.3 The teacher is the manager and director of learning.

Teacher-centred (transmission)

3.   Decision-making.

3.1 Decision-making is a prescribed process which rests with the teacher.

Teacher-centred (transmission)

3.2 Decision-making is made through reflection and consultation and teachers consider a range of factors and dialogue with pupils focuses on equality and social justice.

Constructed communities (transformation)

3.3 Decision-making reflects that teaching is a complex craft and decisions are best made through reflection and consultation with pupils.

Learner-centred (transaction)

4.   The nature of knowledge and knowing.

4.1 Knowledge is dynamic and changing and constructed. Knowing is multi-dimensional and contextual. Dialogue is central to creating a community of learners. Pupils and teachers are co-learners.

Constructed communities (transformation)

4.2 Knowledge is an objective body of information transmitted from teachers to pupils.

Teacher-centred (transmission)

4.3 Knowledge is dynamic and changing and knowing is in relation to the knower. Depth is valued over breadth in the curriculum.

Learner-centred (transaction)

References

Alexander, R. (2008). *Essays on pedagogy*. London: Routledge.

Aronson, E., Blaney, N., Stephan, C., Sikes, J., & Snapp, M. (1978). *The jigsaw classroom*. Beverly Hills, CA: Sage.

Battisch, V., Solomon, D., & Delucci, K. (1993). Interaction process and student outcomes in cooperative learning groups. *The Elementary School Journal, 94*(1), 19–32.

Baumeister, R., Campbell, J., Krueger, J. & Vohs, K. (2003). Does high self-esteem cause better performance, interpersonal success, happiness, or healthier lifestyles? *Psychological Science in the Public Interest, 4*, 1–44.

Berger, J., Fisek, M. H., Norman, R., & Zelditch, M. (1977). *Status characteristics and social interaction*. New York: Elsevier.

Bloom, B. S., Krathwohl, D. R. & Masia, B. B. (1973). *Taxonomy of educational objectives. Handbook I and II*. New York: David McKay Company and Longmans.

Brody, C. M. (1998). The significance of teacher beliefs for professional development and cooperative learning. In: C. M. Brody & N. Davidson (Eds.), *Professional development for cooperative learning: Issues and approaches*, 25–48. Albany, NY: State University of New York Press.

Brody, C. M. & Davidson, N. (Eds.) (1998). *Professional development for cooperative learning: Issues and approaches*. Albany: NY: State University of New York Press.

Bryk, A. & Schneider, B. (2003). Trust in schools: A core resource for school reform. *Educational Leadership, 6*, 40–45.

Callender, A., & McDaniel, M. (2009). The limited benefits of rereading educational texts. *Contemporary Educational Psychology, 34*(1), 30–41.

Cohen, E. G. (1984). Talking and working together: Status interaction and learning. In: P. Peterson; L. C. Wilkinson and M. Hallinan (Eds.), *The social context of instruction: Group organisation and group processes*. 171–187. New York: Academic Press.

Cohen, E. G., (1994). *Designing groupwork: Strategies for the heterogeneous classroom* (2nd edn). New York: Teachers College Press.

Cohen, E. G., and Lotan, R. A. (2014). *Designing groupwork: Strategies for the heterogeneous classroom* (3rd edn). New York: Teachers College Press.

Cohen, E. (1998). Complex Instruction. *European Journal of Intercultural Studies 9*(2), 127–132.

Cohen, E. G. & Lotan, R. A. (1995). Producing equal-status interaction in the heterogeneous classroom. *American Educational Research Journal, 32*(1), 99–120.

Cohen, E. & Lotan, R. (Eds). (1997). *Working for equity in heterogeneous classrooms: Sociological theory in practice*. New York: Teachers College.

Deutsch, M. (1949). An experimental study of the effects of cooperation and competition upon group processes. *Human Relations, 2*, 199–232.

Deutsch, M. (1962). Cooperation and trust: Some theoretical notes. In: M. R. Jones, (Ed), *Nebraska symposium on motivation*, 275–319. Lincoln, NE: University of Nebraska Press.

Dewey, J. (1933). *How we think: A restatement of the relation of reflective thinking to the educative process*. Boston, MA: D.C. Heath.

Dumas, A. (1884). *The three musketeers*. https://en.wikipedia.org/wiki/Project_Gutenberg [accessed 3.4.17].

Ekman, T. (2007). *Demokratisk kompetens: Om gymnasiet som demokratiskola*, Gothenburg: Göteborgs Universitet, Department of Political Science.

Ferguson-Patrick, K. (2008). The values of citizenship in a cooperative classroom: Early career teachers' perspectives. *The Social Educator, 26*, 11–18.

Ferguson-Patrick, K. (2014). *Establishing a democracy classroom: Cooperative learning and good teaching*. PhD: University of Newcastle.

Finnan, C., Schnepel, K. & Anderson, L. (2003). Powerful learning environments: The critical link between school and classroom cultures. *Journal of Education for Students Placed at Risk, 8*, 391–418.

Florian, L. & Black-Hawkins, K. (2011). Exploring inclusive pedagogy. *British Educational Research Journal, 37*, 813–828.

Florian, L. & Linklater, H. (2010). Preparing teachers for inclusive education: Using inclusive pedagogy to enhance teaching and learning for all. *Cambridge Journal of Education, 40*, 369–386.

Galton, M., Hargreaves, L., Comber, C., Wall, D., & Pell, A. (1999). *Inside the primary classroom 20 years on*. London: Routledge.

Gillies, R. (2004). The effects of communication training on teachers' and students' verbal behaviours during cooperative learning. *International Journal of Educational Research, 41*, 257–279.

Gillies, R. (2007). *Cooperative learning: Integrating theory and practice*. London: Sage.

Gillies, R. (2016). *Enhancing classroom-based talk: Blending practice research and theory*. Abingdon: Routledge.

Goleman, D. (2007). *Social intelligence*. London: Arrow.

Greene, M. (1993). The passions of pluralism multiculturalism and the expanding community. *Educational Researcher, 22*(1), 13–18.

Howe, C. & Abedin, M. (2013). Classroom dialogue: A systematic review across four decades of research. *Cambridge Journal of Education, 37*, 325–356.

Johnson, D. W. & Johnson, R. T. (1975). *Learning together and alone: Cooperative, competitive and individualistic learning*. Needham Heights, MA: Allyn and Bacon.

Johnson, D. W. & Johnson, R. (1979). Conflict in the classroom: Controversy and learning. *Review of Educational Research, 49*, 51–70.

Johnson, D. W. & Johnson. R. T. (1989). *Cooperation and competition: Theory and research*. Edina, MN: Interaction Book Company.

Johnson, D. W., Johnson, R. T., & Holubec, E. (1998). *Cooperation in the classroom*. Boston, MA: Allyn and Bacon.

Johnson, D. W., Johnson, R. T., & Holubec, E. J. (1990). *Circles of learning: Cooperation in the classroom* (3rd edn). Edina, MN: Interaction Book Company.

Johnson, D. W. & Johnson, R. T. (1999). *Learning together and alone: Cooperation, competitive and individualistic learning*, (5th edn). Boston, MA: Allyn and Bacon.

Johnson, D. W. & Johnson, R. T. (2008). Social independence theory and cooperative learning: The teacher's role. In: R.B. Gillies, A.F. Ashman, & J. Terwel (Eds), *The teacher's role in implementing cooperative learning in the classroom*, 9–37. New York: Springer.

Johnson, D. W. & Johnson, R. T. (2014). Cooperative learning in the 21st century. *Anales de psicologia, 30*(3), 841–851.

Johnson, D. W. & Johnson, R.T. (2016). Cooperative learning and teaching citizenship in democracies. *International Journal of Educational Research, 76*, 162–177.

Jolliffe, W. (2007). *Cooperative learning in the classroom: Putting it into practice*. London: Sage.

Kagan, S. (1994). *Cooperative learning*. San Juan Capistrano, CA: Kagan Cooperative Learning.

King, A. (2008). Structuring peer interaction to promote higher-order thinking and complex learning in cooperating groups. In: R. Gillies, A. Ashman, & J. Terwel (Eds), *The teacher's role in implementing cooperative learning in the classroom*, 73–91. New York: Springer.

Lewin, K. (1948). *Resolving social conflicts*. New York: Harper.

Lewin, K. (1951, reprinted 1964). *Field theory in social science: Selected theoretical papers by Kurt Lewin*. New York: Harper & Row. (Ed. D. Cartwright) Chapter 7, Problems of research in social psychology (1943–1944) includes part of Lewin 1943 and Lewin 1944.

Lingard, B. & Keddie, A. (2013). Redistribution, recognition and representation: Working against pedagogies of indifference. *Pedagogy, Culture and Society, 21*, 427–447.

Lovat, T. & Toomey, R. (2007). *Values education and quality teaching: The double helix effect*. Terrigal, NSW: David Barlow Publishing.

McCoy, M. L. & Scully, P. L. 2002. Deliberative dialogue to expand civic engagement: What kind of talk does democracy need? *National Civic Review*, (91), 117–135.

Mercer, N. (2008). Talk and the development of reasoning and understanding. *Human Development, 52*, 90–100.

Miller, J. P., & Seller, W. (1985). *Curriculum perspectives and practice*. New York: Longman.

Mills, M. & Gale, T. (2010). *Schooling in disadvantaged communities*. New York: Springer.

Morcom, V. & Cumming-Potvin, W. (2010). Bullies and victims in a primary classroom: Scaffolding a collaborative community of practice. *Issues in Educational Research, 20*(2), 166–182.

Morris, R. (1977). A normative intervention to equalize participation in task-orientated groups. *Unpublished doctoral dissertation*. Stanford, CA: Stanford University.

Nagda, B. A., Gurin, P., & Lopez, G. E. (2003). Transformative pedagogy for democracy and social justice. *Race, ethnicity and education, 6*, 165–191.

NSW Department of Education and Training (2003). *Quality teaching: A classroom practice guide*. Ryde, NSW: Department of Education and Training Professional Support and Curriculum Directorate.

O'Donnell, A.M. (2006). The role of peers and group learning. In: P. A. Alexander & P. H. Winne (Eds), *Handbook of Educational Psychology* (2nd edn), 781–802. Mahwah, NJ: Erlbaum.

Osterman, K. (2000). Students' need for belonging in the school community. *Review of Educational Research, 70*, 323–367.

Palincsar, A. S., Brown, A.L., & Martin, S.M. (1987). Peer interaction in reading comprehension instruction. *Educational Psychologist, 22*, 231–253.

Pescarmona, I. (2015). Status problem and expectations of competence: A challenging path for teachers. *Education 3–13: International Journal of Primary, Elementary and Early Years Education, 43*(1), 30–39,

Piaget, J. (1926). *The language and thought of the child*. New York: Harcourt Brace.

Piaget, J., & Inhelder, B. (1969). *The psychology of the child*. London: Routledge & Kegan Paul.

Ryan, A. & Patrick, H. (2001). The classroom social environment and changes in adolescents' motivation and engagement during middle school. *American Educational Research Journal, 38*, 437–460.

Schmuck, R. & Schmuck, P. (2001). *Group processes in the classroom*. (8th edn). Boston, MA: McGraw Hill.

Sharan, S. (1990). *Cooperative learning: Theory and research*. Westport, CN: Praeger.

Sharan, Y., & Sharan, S. (1992). *Expanding cooperative learning through group investigation*. New York: Teachers College Press.

Sharan, Y. (2010). Cooperative learning for academic and social gains: Valued pedagogy, problematic practice. *European Journal of Education, 45*(2), 300–313.

Schunk, D. (2012). *Learning theories: An educational perspective* (6th edn). Boston, MA: Allyn and Bacon.

Slavin, R. (1987). Cooperative learning: Where behavioural and humanistic approaches to classroom motivation meet. *The Elementary School Journal*, (88), 29–37.

Slavin, R. E. (1994). *Using student team learning* (2nd edn). Baltimore, MD: Johns Hopkins University, Center for Social Organization of Schools.

Slavin, R. E. (1995). *Cooperative learning: Theory, research, and practice*. Boston, MA: Allyn and Bacon.

Slavin, R. E. (2015): Cooperative learning in elementary schools. *Education 3–13: International Journal of Primary, Elementary and Early Years Education*, *43*(1), 5–14

Sporer, N., Brunstein, J., & Kieschke, U. (2009). Improving students' reading comprehension skills: Effects of strategy instruction and reciprocal teaching. *Learning and Instruction*, *19*(3), 272–286.

Thomas, T. & Witenberg, R. (2004). *Love thy neighbours: Racial tolerance among young Australians*. Melbourne: Australian Multicultural Foundation.

Topping, K. J. (1996). Effective peer tutoring in further and higher education: A typology and review of the literature. *Higher Education*, *32*, 321–345.

Topping, K. J., Duran, D. & Van Keer, H. (2016). *Using peer tutoring to improve reading skills: A practical guide for teachers*. Abingdon: Routledge.

Vinterek, M. (2010). How to live democracy in the classroom. *Education Inquiry*, *1*, 367–380.

Vygotsky, L. S. (1962). *Thought and language*. Cambridge, MA: MIT Press.

Vygotsky, L. S. (1978). *Mind in society* (Edited by M. Cole, V. John-Steiner, S. Scribner, & E. Souberman). Cambridge, MA: Harvard University Press.

Vygotsky, L. S. (1934/1987). Thinking and speech (N. Minick, Trans.). In: R. W. Rieber & A. S. Carton (Eds), *The collected works of L. S. Vygotsky: Vol. 1. Problems of general psychology*, 39–285. New York: Plenum Press.

Watkins, C. (2005). *Classrooms as learning communities: What's in it for schools?* Abingdon: Routledge.

Webb, N. M. (2008). Learning in small groups. In T. L. Good (Ed), *21st century education: A reference handbook*, 3–211. Los Angeles, CA: Sage.

Wenger, E. (1998). *Communities of practice: Learning, meaning, and identity*. Cambridge, Cambridge University Press.

2

CASE STUDIES OF COOPERATIVE LEARNING FROM AROUND THE WORLD

Learning objectives for this chapter

By reading this chapter you will develop your understanding of the following:

- that cooperative learning can be explored in different ways in different contexts;
- there are different factors that support and inhibit the development of cooperative learning, related to government priorities and curricula;
- a deeper understanding of the policy contexts of both England and Australia in relation to teaching and learning and cooperative learning;
- that the case studies provide concrete examples of cooperative learning in action, in different ways.

Introduction

This chapter will explore the contexts that support and inhibit the development of cooperative learning in a range of countries, including factors related to government priorities and curricula. We particularly examine the policy contexts in Australia and England where the authors of this book are situated. In Australia the Melbourne Declaration, which set broad educational goals for Australian schooling, has a clear focus on promoting collaboration in Australian schools. In England this focus is less obvious, with the introduction of a new National Curriculum in 2014 that emphasises the individual child's progress rather than more innovative pedagogies, including group work. However, some teachers in England – particularly those in more innovative settings such as academies, that do not have to follow the National Curriculum in England – are able to emphasise the 21st century learning skills of critical thinking, collaboration and creativity, communication, problem-solving and ICT literacy using an International Primary Curriculum (IPC).

The case studies in this chapter come from around the world, not just those schools in Australia and England, and demonstrate the different ways in which teachers and schools have embraced cooperative learning and applied it to their particular context.

Government policy on teaching and learning in Australia

There are a number of factors that either support or inhibit the development of cooperative learning, related to government priorities and curricula in Australia. The *Melbourne declaration on educational goals for young Australians* (Ministerial Council on Education, Employment, Training and Youth Affairs [MCEETYA], 2008) established a strong framework for educating the 21st century Australian student – a framework focused towards collaboration and the ability to work in teams. In Australia, the new Australian Curriculum, developed and based on this declaration, has avowed that there are a number of general capabilities which are integrated into all subject areas in the curriculum. These include learning to, 'negotiate and communicate effectively with others; work in teams, positively contribute to groups and collaboratively make decisions; resolve conflict and reach positive outcomes' (Australian Curriculum Assessment and Reporting Authority [ACARA], 2014:104), which are also key social and academic skills for our 21st century learners. The declaration underscores the importance of children cooperating in schools, stating that successful learners, 'are able to plan activities independently, collaborate, work in teams and communicate ideas' (MCEETYA, 2008:8). The focus on promoting collaboration in Australian schools is therefore very obviously apparent.

However, as Ewing (2012:98) states, a national Australian curriculum replete with a high stakes testing regime and 'a website, My School, with its propensity to create league tables is problematic if an improved quality education for all Australian children is the goal'. Australian curriculum reviewers, Donnelly and Wiltshire, (Australian Government, 2014) further describe the Australian curiculum as, 'monolithic, inflexible and unwieldy' and in particular call for, 'subtantial action to address the overcrowding of the primary curriculum'. As Ewing (2012:102) argues:

> Indeed, if the national curriculum is to connect with students of today and be truly future oriented, it needs to address a broad and integrated approach to knowledge and the development of thinking skills and attributes rather than focus on separate academic disciplines. Without such a change, the Australian curriculum is in serious danger of being obsolete.

The overcrowded primary curriculum is very apparent as it contains three main elements. The first is **discipline-based learning content** from Foundation to Year 6 (ages 4–12) in the primary/elementary years of schooling. This is organised into six key areas: English; Mathematics; Science; Humanities and Social Science; The Arts; and Digital and Design Technologies. Secondly are three cross-curriculum priorities:

Aboriginal and Torres Strait Islander Histories and Cultures; Asia and Australia's Engagement with Asia; and Sustainability, and finally, seven general capabilities which have been interspersed into the Australian syllabi: Literacy; Numeracy; ICT Capability; Critical and Creative Thinking; Personal and Social Capability; Ethical Understanding; and Intercultural Understanding.

Personal and social capability

Developing personal and social capability is the key link to cooperative learning. Personal and social capability encompasses pupils' personal/emotional and social/relational dispositions, intelligences, sensibilities and learning. It develops effective life skills for children, including understanding and handling themselves, their relationships, learning and work. It is widely accepted that a personal and social capability will always include a minimum foundation of the four interrelated and non-sequential organising elements used in the personal and social capability learning continuum (self-awareness, self-management, social awareness and social management). Social management involves pupils in forming strong and healthy relationships, and managing and positively influencing the emotions and moods of others. It includes learning how to cooperate, negotiate and communicate effectively with others, work in teams, make decisions, resolve conflict and resist inappropriate

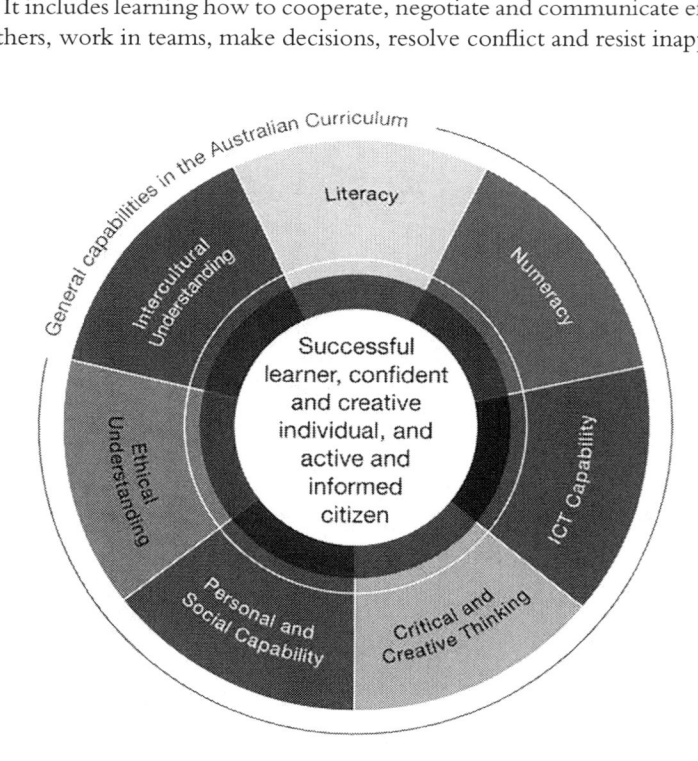

FIGURE 2.1 The seven general capabilities in the Australian curriculum

Source: retrieved on 29.7.17 from www.australiancurriculum.edu.au/f-10-curriculum/general-capabilities

TABLE 2.1 Developing personal and social capability is the key link to cooperative learning: an important focus in Foundation (ages 4–5) to Year 10 (age 16) schooling in Australia (ACARA, 2014).

Personal and Social Capability: Working Collaboratively
Pupils are able to: **Respond to the feelings, needs and interests of others**

Typically by end of Foundation year (age 6)	Share experiences of cooperation in play and group activities.
Typically by end of Year 2 (age 8)	Identify cooperative behaviours in a range of group activities.
Typically by end of Year 4 (age 10)	Describe characteristics of cooperative behaviour and identify evidence of these in group activities.
Typically by end of Year 6 (age 12)	Contribute to groups and teams, suggesting improvements in methods used for group investigations and projects.
Typically by end of Year 8 (age 14)	Assess the extent to which individual roles and responsibilities enhance group cohesion and the achievement of personal and group objectives.
Typically by end of Year 10 (age 16)	Critique their ability to devise and enact strategies for working in diverse teams, drawing on the skills and contributions of team members to complete complex tasks.

Source: Retrieved on 29.7.17 from: www.australiancurriculum.edu.au/f-10-curriculum/general-capabilities/personal-and-social-capability

social pressure. It also involves the ability to initiate and manage successful personal relationships, and participate in a range of social and communal activities. Social management involves building skills associated with leadership, such as working in harmony with others and with shared purpose.

Table 2.1 describes the learning continuum of this particular capability in relation to the working collaboratively element and shows how cooperative learning is an important focus in Foundation (ages 4–5) to Year 10 (age 16) schooling in Australia (ACARA, 2014).

21st century learning

In the past ten years, there has been an upsurge of interest in teaching 21st century skills, but at the same time emphasis on high-stakes testing has meant that teachers have increasingly been fearful of deviating from curriculum guidelines. In primary/ elementary schools in Australia this has meant the main focus has been on teaching literacy and numeracy, usually as discrete units (Gresnigt et al., 2014). Polesel et al. (2014) argued that when the curriculum is taught in this way and such an increasingly competitive and individualistic approach to teaching is taken, there is a risk of it being reduced in both breadth and depth.

This has seen a new emphasis on more competitive ways of learning with a focus on the individual, particularly in response to the increase of high stakes testing (Brand and Triplett, 2012). This has caused much concern for teachers (Polesel et al., 2014) with the range of pedagogies used becoming much more limited

(Reay and William, 1999; Thompson and Harbaugh, 2013), particularly with regard to a reduced emphasis on group work and enquiry-based learning which has been common in Australia.

The testing regime has led to 'scripted pedagogies' in schools (Luke, 2010) which are described as a somewhat reduced and narrowed curriculum as teachers feel the need to teach to the test. This impacts on the type of curriculum offered to children, 'particularly working-class, cultural and linguistic minority students and will deny equality of educational opportunity to such students and thus fail a social democratic reform agenda' (Luke as cited in Lingard, 2010:113). The lack of cooperative learning in classrooms can be explained, in part, by teachers' reluctance to experiment with different pedagogies, especially those using group work, in an environment increasingly focused on individualised testing. Approaches that focus on discrete academic disciplines may not really help to equip our pupils for the creativity and flexibility they need for the 21st century.

Education for the 21st century should develop pupils' skills to allow them to move between workplaces and develop the metacognitive abilities necessary to do this well. These skills are not simply memorisation and repetition but include social skills and attitude sets. The particular way of orienting the self to this 21st century world should include 21st century learning skills, such as critical thinking, communication, collaboration and creativity, problem-solving and ICT literacy, as well as a focus on community. With increased globalisation and digital media, the need to collaborate is more essential as individuals from diverse cultures are exposed to one another (Mishra and Kereluik, 2011).

Government policy on teaching and learning in England

Up until 1988 in England, there had been a history of no central policy direction by government on the curriculum for schools, nor any prescriptive teaching methods. This all changed with the introduction of the National Curriculum, led by a drive for improving standards compared with other countries. This was followed in 1992 by the creation of the Office for Standards in Education (Ofsted) for the inspection of schools. A further key development was the introduction of the National Strategies in 1998 with a detailed framework for teaching literacy and numeracy which set out not only the content to be taught, but also the methods of teaching. This was followed by a series of professional development materials and in 2004, the National Strategies introduced the Excellence and Enjoyment suite (DfES, 2004), which provided guidance on creating the conditions for learning and selecting appropriate pedagogical approaches. Central policy direction, for the first time, acknowledged the importance of talk for learning, and highlighted the use of paired and group work. However, Galton et al.'s (1999) study found classroom practice had shown little change in English primary schools over the previous two decades and curriculum reform had produced a return to whole-class teaching and almost no impact on how teachers organised pupils in classrooms. An extensive ten-year Economic and Social Research Council funded programme,

'Teaching Learning and Research Programme' (TLRP, 2005) culminated in a set of ten principles for effective pedagogy, including promoting learning as a social activity where pupils should be encouraged to work with others, to share ideas and to build knowledge together.

A new National Curriculum came into force in England in 2014, which aims to provide, 'introduction to the essential knowledge that they need to be educated citizens' (DfE, 2013:6). The curriculum sets out detailed programmes of study of what should be taught according to different key stages or year groups, with clear expectations of achievement. However, as with the previous iterations of the national curriculum, it provides no specific guidance on how these programmes should be taught. The focus on skills development and raising expectations of technical aspects of English is more conducive to a focus on traditional didactic teaching. While other countries are focusing on 21st century skills, which would put cooperative group work as a key strategy, England continues to focus on the individual child's progress with measures of accountability for schools, leading to a reluctance to explore alternative pedagogies.

The drive for schools to become academies is a further key policy direction in England. Academies are independent, state-funded schools, which receive their funding directly from central government rather than through a local authority. While the directive for all schools to convert has been dropped from the latest legislation, there is a clear demand for schools who are clearly 'failing' to do so. Academies do not have to follow the National Curriculum in England and there is evidence of some individual academies and larger academy chains exploring different pedagogies, as can be seen in Case study 1 in Goole in the north of England, where the school uses an IPC. Interestingly, one particular development has been the growth of schools becoming cooperative trust schools. The model is membership-based with people from the stakeholder groups becoming members of the 'educational cooperative' for the school or cluster of schools. These schools adopt cooperative values and the method offers schools the opportunity to involve the wider community in the running of the school, including local people, businesses, voluntary groups, charities, parents, pupils and staff through membership of a council or forum. However, to date, this has not led to the widespread adoption of cooperative learning pedagogy – there are a few exceptions, such as the school cited in Case study 2.

Case studies

We have collected a number of case studies from around the world to demonstrate different contextual uses of cooperative learning in other countries and in varying types of schools or contexts. These include:

- a primary school in the north of England;
- a cooperative academy secondary school in the city of Plymouth in the south of England;

- a number of different schools in Sweden, including one in the south of the country using a 'storyline' approach, two in Lund in Skåne, a large primary/middle/high school just outside Stockholm that has a population of children where 70% have Swedish as a second language, and another school just outside Stockholm;
- a school in Hong Kong with a reformed curriculum using cooperative learning in a particular primary class after the school faced closure;
- a small multicultural, inclusive school in India;
- a music teacher in Singapore using cooperative learning;
- a primary school using Complex Instruction (CI), in a village in the Apennines in the Province of Bologna, Italy;
- two schools in Australia; one whose teacher has taught in two non-government schools in New South Wales and one school in the Northern Territory with an Aboriginal population.

Case study 1: Boothferry Primary School, Goole, England

The first case study examined in the book is from an average sized primary school in the north of England for pupils aged 5–11, in a small town called Goole, 30 minutes' drive from the city of Hull, in Yorkshire. The school utilises the International Primary Curriculum (IPC), which is a comprehensive, thematic, creative curriculum for 5–12 year olds, with a clear process of learning and specific learning goals for every subject, for international mindedness and for personal learning. The IPC is the fastest growing independent primary curriculum in the world and is now used by more than 250,000 pupils in 92 countries. It has over 130 different thematic units of learning which tap into children's interests, are internally relevant, and which help them to learn more about and engage positively with the world around them. Organising units around a theme helps children to see 'the big picture' of their learning, make connections through and across different subjects, and talk about a theme from multiple perspectives. The IPC emphasises personal goals, and these underpin those individual qualities and learning dispositions children will find essential in the 21st century: enquiry, resilience, morality, communication, thoughtfulness, cooperation, respect and adaptability (www.greatlearning.com/ipc). Annette's class of Year 6 pupils thrive on her cooperative and inclusive approach, particularly with such a large number of children who have English as an additional language and often have limited English skills when they arrive. She knows how well cooperative learning supports these children, as they are able to talk in small groups and gain confidence in a supportive environment where peers learn through teaching each other.

The context

Goole is an inland port with a population of approximately 20,000. The town has long associations with Eastern European countries and more recently has seen a considerable increase in immigrant population, now estimated to be about 10% of the population of the town. The area suffers from considerable economic deprivation, ranking among the worst 20% in England.

Boothferry school is above average size, with 389 pupils, although it was originally built for 200 pupils and has had to have temporary mobile classrooms to accommodate the increase in size. Forty-three per cent of pupils are entitled to free school meals (an indicator of family poverty which is judged to be high). Thirty-nine per cent of pupils have English as an additional language and in some year groups it is over 50%. In total, 18 languages are spoken; a large number being Eastern European, including Polish, Latvian, Russian, Lithuanian, and Bulgarian. Another feature of the school is the transient nature of the pupils who frequently join the school in later year groups, often speaking little or no English. After an armed services school, the school is the second most transient school in the region.

The senior leadership of the school, which is new in the last three years, has made considerable efforts to raise standards and maintain stability, particularly in reducing the turnover of staff and mitigating a previous reliance on temporary supply teachers. The school has been developing its curriculum to meet the needs of its pupils. The motto of the school is 'Boothferry Primary: Learning Together'.

Background and rationale for introducing cooperative learning

The school is part of a learning community of schools that uses the IPC. This curriculum has a strong element of internationalism built into learning and encourages everyone to collaborate as an essential feature. The school's core values are cooperation, enquiry, resilience, adaptability, thoughtfulness, respect, communication and morality. Cooperative learning, therefore, provides a powerful medium to support these values. Although used across the world, there are few schools in England using this curriculum.

The implementation of cooperative learning has been led over three years by a Year 6 teacher, Annette. Annette, who was introduced to cooperative learning in her training, has developed her practice in two schools. She has led training and workshops for staff, ensuring opportunities for experiencing cooperative learning during these sessions, and she provides ongoing support for teachers to develop this pedagogy.

Cooperative learning in practice

Annette first learned about cooperative learning during her initial teacher training and became particularly interested in this approach, leading to her studying it greater depth. She was fortunate to be in a school on her first school placement that had been part of the Talk for Learning Project which has many common features with cooperative learning and uses 'dialogic teaching' to enhance the power of classroom talk as a tool for learning and teaching. Annette witnessed first-hand the potential of talk to engage and motivate children and to support their learning.

She developed this further and in another placement, she used cooperative learning with mixed ability groups. Although the class teacher she was placed with showed reluctance at first, the impact was soon apparent, particularly on the confidence of the lower ability children in mathematics. In her first post, she continued to make use of cooperative learning, although again it was not common practice in the school. However, the deputy headteacher was so impressed by her work with the class, she asked Annette to lead training with other staff in the school. This she undertook and further developed her own practice as well as supporting other staff. She found that some staff were very keen, but others tried cooperative learning to a more limited extent as they were reluctant to fundamentally change their practice.

At Boothferry, Annette was asked by the headteacher to introduce all the staff to this pedagogy when she arrived three years ago. The headteacher had heard about cooperative learning at a meeting, where it was emphasised how important it was that children work cooperatively, and when he observed Annette teaching prior to her starting at the school, he became keen to introduce this approach. As a result, Annette carried out some training soon after she started at the school and staff began teaching in this way. She followed this up with additional training in mathematics, which received an enthusiastic response as staff felt they could apply it immediately. Annette has ensured that any training was undertaking through staff experiencing cooperative learning strategies first-hand. This has been followed up by workshops after school looking at strategies such as 'solve and switch', 'show down' and 'maths buddies' which staff could use in their classes and prepare suitable resources. A popular structure used across the school is 'Quiz, Quiz, Trade' (see: www.theteachertoolkit.com/index.php/tool/quiz-quiz-trade).

When Annette started teaching her current class, the children were familiar with some of the cooperative strategies, indicating they had been using them in a previous class. She feels that it is becoming embedded in the school and staff have approached her to tell her about things they have tried. This could be developed further if she had more time out of her own class to work with other teachers.

Success with her own classes over this time has further embedded Annette's own practice. At an inspection by Ofsted, she had been observed teaching and the inspector commented that he really liked the focus on talk and that she was asking the children to discuss things. At a recent inspection by the local authority, the use of cooperative learning strategies to support reasoning in mathematics was highlighted again, such as 'solve and switch' (see: www.teacherspayteachers.com/Product/Solve-and-Switch-Freebie-Double-Digit-Multiplication-2293227) and 'numbered heads' (see Appendix 1), which demonstrated how well the children were explaining things to each other. In the recommendations in the written report it stated that the rest of the school should be using similar practice in teaching mathematics.

Annette ensures that she includes team building activities as a starting point with each class she teaches. She feels that although some initial activities are required, this does not take very long and is reinforced during other lessons. In addition, the use of 'circle time' supports this as it provides a time for listening to each other, promoting oral communication and empathy. Circle Time is a teaching strategy which allows the teacher to explore issues of concern. It provides a structured mechanism for solving problems, in which all participants have an equal footing. Circle Time also affords the opportunity for the teacher and class to communicate with each other about issues which promote self-esteem and positive behaviour (see: www.unrwa.org/sites/default/files/introducing_circle_time.pdf).

Annette also uses restorative practice, where children who feel they have been harmed in some way convey the impact to those responsible, who acknowledge the impact and take steps to put it right. The restorative practice approach focuses on repairing harm through inclusive processes that engage all stakeholders. Implemented well, it shifts the focus of discipline from punishment to learning and from the individual to the community (see: www.restorativejustice4schools.co.uk). This helps children who have problems getting along with others. Once the cooperative skills are in place, Annette finds children enjoy working in this way and they do not sit back and let others do the work because they like the challenge and want to take part. She feels that younger children may require more time and support in developing the necessary skills of working together.

Annette uses a range of cooperative learning strategies. She regularly uses numbered heads for children to demonstrate their understanding. For example, when answering a quiz, such as one about grammar, pupils first write down their own answers and put their thumbs up when they are ready – if they are ready before anybody else they explain their answer and think about how they are going to teach it to the rest of their group. They then stand up and put their heads together and discuss it. They often have a time limit to agree a group answer and the children like it when there is a horn or something similar to indicate time is up. They may then alter their own answer and write down the group answer. Annette tells the children they must make sure that everyone understands, as they don't know who is going to be asked to explain. They then get a bonus point for the team for explaining it well. This is also used with the structure 'two stay and two stray', or 'one stray', (see Appendix 1), where pupils have to explain something to another group, again with bonus points for good explanations.

Annette finds the jigsaw structure complements the work with numbered heads as pupils are learning they have a responsibility to carry out their task and become an expert. She does not find this complex to implement and work in expert groups prepares pupils to go back to their home teams and teach each other, emphasising the importance of supporting and encouraging each other in that group. She finds in this way, children are engaged and enjoy this way of working.

One strategy Annette uses, to reward teams for their work together, is to pick a prize from a box using raffle tickets. Prizes include things such as going early to lunch or, one of the most popular, to 'be the teacher'. One team picked this recently and they planned and carried out an activity to create a creature in groups with 'teaching assistants' to support them, which focused on team-building. Because the children understand what teamwork looks like, they had to score each other's teams and the activity worked very well.

One of the most powerful aspects of working in cooperative teams Annette has found, is the way in which peers learn through teaching each other. She cited an example of a school visit where the children visited a seaside resort. Having worked with the children beforehand using jigsaw activities examining some key aspects, the children were delighted to find that they knew a considerable amount of the information they heard on the visit, chorusing excitedly, 'We know this!'. The level of recall was clearly due to the children having taught each other about it. This was in marked contrast to other children from different classes who also took part in the trip.

As well as improving pupils' learning, Annette has found the impact has been very much on communication skills and children are regularly building these skills through mini-debates, where they work with a few other children, developing their confidence to make presentations later to the whole class. Other 21st century skills, such as creativity, are enhanced for example in mathematics, where pupils are thinking creatively about how to solve problems and this is helping their critical thinking. Cooperation skills are a key feature, assisted by the emphasis on team-building. Teams are used according to the particular lesson and subject and not established over a lengthy time. Sometimes roles are used in groups, and children are always in mixed ability groups to help develop the confidence of less able pupils.

The impact on inclusion is marked, particularly in Boothferry. Annette feels cooperative learning supports children with English as an additional language, as they are able to talk in small groups, gain confidence and have support, rather than speak in front of the whole class, thereby taking the pressure off. Annette cited one particular example of a boy who barely spoke English when he started and had no self-confidence. She explained:

> Previously he had worked with a Teaching Assistant (TA) as anyone who starts school who has no English, they have a TA who works specifically with them. At first, this child thought 'I can't do that' so he didn't really try, he didn't really speak, he didn't write, he didn't do anything and wouldn't work with other children. He would have struggled in his own country, they were all those sorts of barriers for him. But the different groups I put him in over the year has helped him realise he can work with other children he would never put himself with, or never choose to talk to, and never worked with before . . . he came up to me the other week and I think because of doing this and having to work cooperatively and he said 'when I came to this class I could do nothing' and dancing about while he is telling me 'but now I can do all sorts of things, I can do this, I can write, I can . . .' he was so excited. It is things like that when you see it has had a big impact.

From this, and particularly in the context of the children in this school, it has become clear that cooperative learning provides an inclusive pedagogy for a diverse society.

Next steps

Annette is now moving to another school to take up a more senior role. At her interview for the post, and from the observation of her teaching by the headteacher of this school, her use of cooperative learning was highlighted as good practice and the school is keen for her to develop this in her new post. She feels it is a key part of her professional identity as a teacher and would find it essential to use. Her work in sharing and developing this practice at Boothferry Primary School has helped other staff and it is now part of the development plan for the school. This clearly supports the school ethos to encourage everyone to collaborate and to build internationalism into learning.

Case study provided by: Mrs Annette Woodhouse, Year 6 Teacher, Mathematics Lead, Boothferry Primary School, Goole, UK.

Questions for reflection

1. How does restorative practice help Annette build the skills of cooperative learning in her classroom?
2. Consider how cooperative learning has been beneficial for those children for whom English is an additional language.
3. How does this school use the International Primary Curriculum to develop 21st century learning skills?

Case study 2: Lipson Co-operative Academy School, England

Lipson Co-operative Academy School is a large secondary school in the city of Plymouth, Devon. It has an entire educative project based around cooperative learning and underpinned by the values of the cooperative movement which have been adapted to suit the Lipson context: Self-help, Self-responsibility, Democracy, Equality, Equity, Solidarity, Honesty, Openness, Social Responsibility and Caring for Others.

The context

Lipson is situated in an urban inner-city location. The age range of the school's 1,084 children is 11–18; 262 take 16–19 years programmes.

Background and rationale for introducing cooperative learning

Lipson Co-operative Academy School is a single school foundation trust established in 2011. Lipson operates in partnership with a local consortium of non-cooperative schools – the Partnership for Learning and Education. The school was already operating in a cooperative and collaborative manner before taking on the status of a cooperative school. This meant that taking on a formal cooperative structure did not involve a fundamental change in the nature of the school.

Cooperative learning in practice

Cooperative learning is the organising principle for teaching and learning at Lipson.

The school has organised its entire educative project around cooperative learning, defining the curriculum, the classroom strategies and the school's design (including classroom seating arrangements) accordingly. This commitment to cooperative learning is stated on the school's website (see www.lipsonco-opera tiveacademy.coop/Statement-on-the-Co-operative-Identity).

> Cooperative learning is a structured and disciplined approach that encourages dialogue and promotes confidence in the learner. It involves deep thinking and active participation that students find challenging and motivational. A cooperative classroom is one that relies on open and constructive dialogue.
>
> *(Lipson Academy information)*

This commitment to cooperative learning is consolidated and carried out by a structured and well thought through approach to group learning, where groups of pupils are made up with different levels of ability so that they can learn from each other. Almost all the classrooms have non-conventional seating arrangements, where instead of rows the classrooms are arranged for group work. Usually, there are four pupils per group. All the classes are organised around group or peer exercises. The pupils work on the exercise and the teachers act more like facilitators of the process. The idea is that the pupils can help each other before the teacher needs to intervene. This approach gives great importance to self-learning, which is achieved with the support of other children and the teacher.

Many classroom exercises foster collaboration and the sharing of knowledge. For example, in the music class the teacher encouraged the pupils to teach each other the functions of the software they were studying. In a maths class, the pupils worked in groups and replied to some exercises written on cards. Here, the teacher encouraged the mutual support of the children.

There is a strong commitment at Lipson to the ethos and values of the cooperative movement. The children are aware of these values and their significance on how the school is organised, including the positive ways they impact on their own learning. These values of the cooperative movement have been adapted to suit the Lipson context. The impression is that these cooperative principles engender a strong commitment to teaching and to learning among staff and pupils.

The process of implementing cooperative learning across the school was initially problematic. In the beginning, it adopted a prescriptive top-down approach, but this has now become a much more organic process for pupil learning as well personal and professional development of the teachers, allowing for professional discretion and judgement.

The teachers embrace a cooperative model in the planning and assessment of their classes. Through CPD programmes and other teachers' meetings, they are able to share their strategies in the classroom and the pupils' progress. In this way, they are not only individuals trying their best to deliver a good class, but are part of a team of teachers who care for each other and who want the best for their pupils and colleagues.

There is a strong connection between cooperative learning and cooperative leadership at Lipson. Cooperative learning is described as a process where pupils know that they have roles within each learning group so they can drive up each other's learning as part of a very positive set of relationships, improving their progress. Following on from this, cooperative leadership is an outcome of this process of cooperative learning, but at the level of the institution. Staff and pupils in the school recognise the significance of their interdependent roles, trusting and relying on each other to make decisions at the appropriate level for the benefit of the whole school.

This structured approach to pupils learning from each other carries over into the way in which the school organises its Guilds – a distinctive feature of Lipson. The school has five Guilds, each with a unique identity but all based on cooperative values and principles. The Guilds are organised around subject specialisms: Chandlers – sport and health; Surfers – maths, ICT and technology; Mariners – English, communications and modern foreign languages; Merchants: science, ethics and humanities; and Players – visual and performing arts and creative media. Each Guild is divided into tutor groups with 20 children made up from all levels across the school.

Next steps

The principles and practices of cooperative learning are already well embedded within the school. The school is constantly looking for ways to improve its pedagogical practices through a range of processes that include formal and informal dialogue with pupils, collaborative Professional Development programmes as well as research-based evidence. A feature of Lipson is the support for teachers to undertake post-graduate research in education at local universities. Research topics include leading change in the curriculum, pupil engagement, pastoral interventions, participation in physical activity by boys and girls, and perceptions of mathematics. This means the school has a substantial foundation on which to base its work to support and develop a progressive form of cooperative teaching and learning, and to foster innovative styles of pedagogy.

Case study provided by: Mike Neary, Professor of Sociology, University of Lincoln

Questions for reflection

1. In what ways has the school demonstrated a commitment to cooperative learning?
2. What links are there between cooperative learning and cooperative leadership at the school?
3. Consider the values of the cooperative movement and how they relate to the development of the 21st century learner.

Cooperative learning in Sweden

The third, fourth and fifth case studies are all set in Sweden, where there is some promotion of group learning in the curriculum but no guidance for teachers on how cooperative learning should be implemented. The Swedish curriculum does advocate cooperation, communication and democratic values, which fits well with cooperative learning.

Case study 3: The Storyline approach, Sweden

The first of the Swedish case studies uses an integrated curriculum approach called **Storyline** (see: www.storyline-scotland.com/what-is-storyline-2). Storyline uses the basic elements of 'story' – setting, characters and plot – to frame the learning plan. This approach has been in existence in Scotland since the 1960s and was first introduced to encourage environmental education and awareness. The Senior Lecturer from Kristianstad University who has researched the use of this approach, outlines a storyline topic focused on sustainability, aimed at how we can we live in a more environmentally friendly way, with a class of 32 11–13 year olds. The storyline approach has been used widely throughout the world including Scandinavia, Iceland, the Netherlands, Germany, The United States, Thailand and Singapore.

The context

In the south of Sweden there is a small online-based network for teachers interested in cooperative learning, with occasional meetings in schools for members to share ideas and experiences. However, although pupil cooperation within groups is advocated across the curriculum, there is no guidance for teachers on what form this cooperation might take or how it should be implemented.

Background and rationale for introducing cooperative learning

The focus of this case study is on the impact of the Storyline approach on the English language development of upper primary aged children, from 11–13 years. The rationale for this was that the word most commonly used by pupils of all ages to describe working with Storyline is 'fun'. In her role as researcher, Sharon's ambition for the study was to find out what it was about this approach to which the pupils responded well and to investigate how this impacted on their learning of English, which they had started at the age of seven. In their usual English lessons, younger and older pupils were taught separately, which was also the case for mathematics. For other subjects, they were taught together. Although the older pupils occasionally read and worked with fiction in the form of short stories and novels in their English lessons, most of the time all the pupils were taught traditionally with textbooks and workbooks.

Storyline is an interdisciplinary teaching approach, which integrates practical and theoretical subjects. Today it is implemented at different age levels and in both first and second language teaching contexts throughout the world.

The characteristic features of Storyline are that pupils work closely in small groups to build a fictitious world, in which they create and take on the role of characters in a story. The story develops as the children work on open key questions, which drive the story forward, presenting pupils with incidents or problems requiring action on their part. Pupils' work is displayed on a frieze, which charts the unfolding story, and a story might typically last between four and six weeks.

Cooperative learning in practice with Storyline

This study involved one class of 32 children, aged 11–13, and two teachers (for more detail, see Ahlquist, 2013). It took place over a five-week period in a village school with about 500 pupils aged 6–16, for two hours, four days a week. The Storyline approach had previously been used at this school in both first and second language teaching.

The story involved the pupils working in groups of four, as families who had moved into a new street in a fictitious English town. Each group consisted of two younger and two older pupils and the aim was to have a balance of the sexes, though this was not always possible.

The pupils created characters for these families (drawing self-portraits of the character rather than making models, which they had done in a previous Storyline), and introduced them both orally and in the form of a written description and diary of their character's typical day. The pupils drew pictures of their new home and wrote an estate agent's advertisement for it. The families took part in a project to live in a more sustainable way, and dealt with the problems of outsiders dumping rubbish in their street, as well as the issue of anti-social neighbours, before the story ended with a street party. A celebratory event to bring the story to a happy conclusion and draw a line under the period of work is a characteristic feature of Storyline.

A frieze is also developed to build up the story. This plays an important part in bringing the jointly constructed world to life. Each family has a piece of green A4 paper to represent their plot of land, then the house description and the self-portraits are put up around these. The point of the frieze is that it is a product of pupils' collaboration and it shows the story to date. The teacher or the pupils can create quizzes based on the information displayed, and because it presents a record of what has been done in the class and by the class, it is an aid to learning as well as a source of pride.

The key questions which structured this Storyline were:

1. Who are you?
2. What is your house like?
3. How can we live in a more environmentally friendly way?
4. What can we do about the rubbish problem in our street?
5. What can we do about the problem with the new neighbours?
6. How can we celebrate a year of living in our street?

In addition to the syllabus for English, in which the pupils were developing their communication skills as well as their knowledge of grammar and vocabulary, content from the syllabi for art, civics and natural science was also incorporated. The pupils had previously worked with the science content in their first language, but now they were learning English words for familiar concepts and applying their existing knowledge in the Storyline problems.

Data collection tools used to assess the impact were: questionnaires, learner journals, observation notes, interviews with a number of both pupils and teachers, audio and video sequences and samples of the pupils' written work throughout the study. The results demonstrated an increased willingness to speak English; improved ability to understand the teachers' spoken English; greater certainty in the use of some grammatical structures; many new words; longer and more complex written texts; and greater confidence in reading.

The pupils' most commonly used word to describe their Storyline experience was 'fun'. Features that were popular included, 'variety, not working with the textbook, and not knowing what was coming next'. The two most popular aspects of the project were 'integrating artwork with English' and also 'working in groups', which the pupils were not used to doing in English. The reasons included, 'being with friends, being able to get help in the group and working in a group is more fun than doing something on your own'. However, where the group did not work well, due to personality conflicts, the response was less positive – this was especially so for pupils who generally preferred to work alone, those who felt that they achieved better results on their own or those who preferred the security of their textbook. The teachers saw two specific benefits as a result of group cooperation, stating, 'the less proficient pupils persevered where they would have given up if working alone; the more proficient of the younger pupils were pushed to perform by working with older pupils in the group'. When the pupils were asked to explain the factors, which contributed to good or poor group cooperation, the most commonly stated reason was that, 'some members of the group attempted to dominate'. With hindsight, Sharon commented it would have been useful at the halfway stage, not only to ask the pupils to predict how they thought the story might develop based on what had happened so far, but also to discuss with them the consequences of their own and others' behaviour for the effectiveness of both the group's and their own individual work, then to ask them to formulate an agreement for going forward. This could then have been evaluated at the end of the study.

What was clear was that for many pupils, the sense of being part of a group within Storyline went deeper than collaborating with peers. In their evaluations, many pupils wrote about their group as the 'family'. The girls in particular were motivated by creating a character, or a family, and then being that person. This was part of the 'fun' and they were clear that, to quote one pupil, 'the more fun it is the more you learn'. This mirrors Hattie's (2009) conclusion that achievement is higher where there is enjoyment. The affective dimension to the nature of group work in Storyline can thus be said to have the potential to touch pupils on a deeper level than in other kinds of collaboration, enhancing learning as a result.

All of the skills for the 21st century of collaboration, communication, creativity and innovation – critical thinking, problem-solving, learning to learn, ICT and literacy, flexibility, adaptability and initiative, global awareness and citizenship – are integrated within Storyline.

Case study provided by: Sharon Ahlquist, Senior Lecturer, Kristianstad University, Sweden

Questions for reflection

1. Discuss how the Storyline approach can work well for pupils with English as a second or additional language.
2. Consider how Storyline can complement cooperative group work.
3. What could the school do about those pupils who may want to *dominate* the activity?

Case study 4: Fäladsskolan and Delfinskolan schools, Sweden

The fourth case study, also set in the south of Sweden, in Lund, Skåne, describes the work undertaken by two primary schools who were involved with a series of professional learning opportunities led by a consultant. They are currently introducing more cooperative learning strategies in their classrooms as a result of this professional learning and are keen to share their experiences with other teachers in the region.

The context

Lund has a population of 100,000 and the town is known for its university. Fäladsskolan is a multicultural school located in the northern part of Lund with a mixed variety of nationalities and socio-economic conditions. The school has about 250 children aged 10–12 and each class has about 25 pupils. Delfinskolan has 85 children aged 6–9 years old. Each class has about 15–20 pupils. Both schools are located in the same area.

Cooperative learning fits well with the Swedish curriculum. In most single subjects, pupils need to show and share knowledge, thoughts, ideas and experiences by communicating with each other in different group sizes. Asking questions and verbally communicating their understanding in a subject is one of many aspects in which pupils are assessed.

The Swedish curriculum also contains a more general section that describes the 'beliefs and values' all children in Sweden should develop during the compulsory years in school. Here, cooperative learning fits very well in the development of social skills such as, for example, cooperation, respect, tolerance, creativity, curiosity, communication, etc. Everyone working in a Swedish school has a responsibility to work on developing this.

Background and rationale for introducing cooperative learning

At a conference in 2014 one of the teachers was introduced to cooperative learning while visiting different schools in London. During these visits, she noticed several similarities between the classrooms, for example, classroom management, methods, vocabulary and furniture. She also noticed that the pupils seemed to talk and listen to each other at the same time as they were active and busy with the planned activity.

This was something Swedish schools were looking for: methods, strategies, a consensus they could all work with and develop. Another teacher had worked in International Baccalaureate schools, where she had come across cooperative learning in different ways. As a result, both teachers decided they would like to find out more about cooperative learning, both for themselves and for their colleagues, and they found a consultant in Sweden who could educate them.

Staff from three schools had lectures and workshops for ten hours during the first semester. In semester two they had ten more hours of training and on top of that also one hour each of tutorial with the consultant. Between the workshops, they had homework such as reading, discussion and practising some cooperative learning structures.

Cooperative learning in practice

The teachers began by dividing the pupils into heterogeneous teams with between three and five pupils in each team. These teams were kept together for about six to eight weeks.

During the first semester, they worked a lot with cooperative skills with several teachers trying to use the cooperative structures they learned during the workshops and implement them in the classroom. The focus was on social skills, not the knowledge.

The curriculum stresses cooperation between the pupils and teachers often asked them to work together on projects, but without giving them the tools to learn and understand how to cooperate. Teachers can see that the methods and strategies they have worked with in cooperative learning help their pupils to become better at cooperating. Their pupils understand that cooperation requires skills that they can develop and that these affect their knowledge in a subject. While the pupils are active using a structure, they as teachers found it easier to see and hear every pupil. They could walk around in the classroom and hear how they discussed things together and explained things to each other. They had time to hear more than one pupil at a time. They found it easier to walk in between classrooms and teach when they knew that all pupils were familiar with the vocabulary and methods.

Next steps

From autumn 2016 two teachers have been responsible for cooperative learning in the two schools. Their responsibilities are, for example: discussions between teachers; educating new staff; tutorials for staff; and inspiring, sharing and communicating experience and knowledge about cooperative learning to other schools. They are planning to continue to develop this work.

Case study provided by: Anette Swartling and Anna Andersson, teachers, Fäladsskolan and Delfinskolan, Lunds kommun, Sweden

Questions for reflection

1. What kinds of cooperative skills do you think the teachers may have worked on at these schools?
2. One of the features here, is of one or two teachers becoming experts and then supporting other teachers in their schools. Consider how effective this is as a method of professional development.
3. What steps did the schools take to ensure they were more aware of the strategies and theory behind cooperative learning?

Case study 5: Västerholms Friskola, Sweden

The fifth case study is set just outside the capital Stockholm, in a multi-ethnic and culturally rich area with many new arrival or refugee pupils. In the school about 90% of the pupils speak two or more languages and 70% of pupils have Swedish as a second language. The success gained from using cooperative learning in these classrooms is apparent as the teachers claim their pupils are showing more flexibility when it comes to working with different people and are quicker in accepting individual differences. There is obviously a thriving community of teachers using cooperative learning in Sweden as their blog (https://kooperativt.com) had 500,000 hits in just over a year.

The context

The school is located in Skärholmen, a suburb of Stockholm some 25 kilometres south of the city centre. The district has a high percentage of foreign-born children or children with two foreign-born parents. According to statistics from Stockholm city, over 80% have a different background than Swedish, of which more than half are originally from outside the EU's borders. Skärholmen is considered a multi-ethnic and culturally rich area. Most of the schools in the area receive newly arrived children that have a need for an identity and affinity with the new country they have moved to. Many have fled war and unrest with nothing more than what they could carry on their backs. Some children have never had the opportunity to go to school and some have never even been outside their family house before arriving in Sweden. Västerholms Friskola has some 800 pupils aged 6–15 (primary/middle/high school). Class size is between 16–22 pupils. About 90% of the children speak two or more languages and 70% have Swedish as a second language. This is a great source of knowledge and learning resource, but also a challenge for teachers to help the pupils reach the goals in the national curriculum in all of their school subjects.

The Swedish curriculum includes cooperation, communication and democratic values, which fits well with cooperative learning.

Background and rationale for introducing cooperative learning

One thing we all have in common as human beings is the need to talk and share experiences. Early on the teachers could see that it was impossible to reach the goals in the national curriculum with some pupils barely being able to speak Swedish, and others who had been talking and reading books in the language since birth. The diversity of knowledge in Swedish and school backgrounds made it impossible for traditional teacher-centred learning strategies. Teachers wanted children to be active, to interact with each other, to learn together and bridge the achievement gap. They wanted them to help each other. That's when they started practising cooperative learning in their classrooms.

Cooperative learning in practice

It all started as a project between colleagues where they expanded the 'think-pair-share' strategy and started doing pair work between pupils in the classroom. Three colleagues then gathered staff and had workshops where they used cooperative strategies in staff meetings. Each week they tested new things and new ideas in their classrooms, transforming the teacher-centred approach to a pupil-centred one, with cooperative structures and strategies. They started a blog together that in just a few months had more than 200,000 visits (500,000 after a year). Many teachers around Sweden were now trying cooperative structures and group work in their classrooms.

Early on teachers could see a huge impact on different variables with their own pupils, such as attention, achievement and positive peer relationships. Having pupils work in pairs and teams also made them like school more and made pupils with autism and ADHD more included in the classroom. Cooperative learning engaged their pupils and learning no longer seemed boring or tedious. The number of pupils who needed to leave the classroom for special education sessions dropped significantly in the classrooms that used cooperative learning, which was also a sign that it worked wonders for their multi-ethnic and multicultural children. This was even more apparent with pupils who were newly arrived and couldn't speak Swedish: they quickly had multiple opportunities to communicate with their classmates and through cooperative structures, they got to hear phrases and words several times and then tried to use them for themselves. Their team mates, who were more fluent in Swedish, learned to use their whole body as a communication tool – they pointed, described and drew on mini-whiteboards and explained their own learning to each other. Pupils started to invest in their fellow classmates' learning. They were now teaching each other and helping each other just as teachers wanted them to do.

Peer learning changed the role of the teacher. Instead of lecturing and helping individual pupils the teacher now had to facilitate the learning process and teach interpersonal skills so that the pupils could learn more together. The teachers now moved around the classroom and observed the children, only intervening when necessary. This way, the knowledge the pupils had was made visible for the teacher right away, and the teacher could plan accordingly.

The pupils who worked with cooperative learning showed more flexibility when it came to working with different people and were quicker in accepting people's differences. They also focused more on the task at hand than on who they are working with, which made personal conflicts fewer and easier to deal with. Working cooperatively had improved the relationships between the pupils and helped them make more friends. Their critical thinking had improved as they were required to put their thoughts into words and explain themselves to others.

Teaching cooperatively has also changed the way the classrooms are set up. Now they are furnished to facilitate cooperation and group work. Instead of rows of tables facing the front of the room, the tables are pushed to the sides and taken out when needed. A group of four can work around one small table instead of having four tables pushed together, to help them get closer together as they work. There is a better flow in the classroom as they move from class work, to pair work, to group work and back to class work. The seats are not static and assigned to one specific pupil (unless a pupil with special needs requires that); instead the pupils can use the room for different things at different times.

Next steps

In autumn 2017, cooperative learning was implemented in all classes from Year 0 to Year 3. A project group with members from each year was formed and led by a teacher who had worked with cooperative learning for some time. Workshops and pedagogical forums were held continually to assess the progress and set new

FIGURE 2.2 Roundtable activity with students writing collaboratively

goals. Niclas, Jennie, Lisa and a colleague from the south of Sweden have also written a book about cooperative learning: *Grundbok i kooperativt lärande. Vägen till det samarbetande klassrummet* (Beginning book on cooperative learning: The way to the collaborative classroom). Niclas, Jennie and Lisa also continue to hold workshops in schools in and around Stockholm to spread cooperative learning to other schools. They also work with others who work cooperatively and who work at spreading their knowledge around the country. An organisation for cooperative learning in Sweden, Kooperativt Lärande i Sverige (KOLiS) (https://kooperativt.com), has also been started. They plan to hold conferences and facilitate learning between teachers in Sweden who use, or are interested in using, cooperative learning in their classrooms.

Case study provided by: Niclas Fohlin, Jennie Wilson and Lisa Westman, teachers and colleagues, Västerholms Friskola

Questions for reflection

1. Discuss the impact the teachers saw on their pupils when using cooperative learning.
2. Consider how the teachers have moved furniture to facilitate cooperative learning.
3. Note how a group of teachers within the school is responsible for leading and providing ongoing opportunities to learn more about cooperative learning and consider the impact of this.

Case study 6: Lok Sin Tong Leung Wong Wai Fong Memorial School, Hong Kong

This case study is based in Hong Kong and is written by an Associate Professor from The Education University of Hong Kong. Since Hong Kong became a British colony in the nineteenth century, the curriculum has been examination-oriented. Pupils faced a very keen competition in the different stages of their learning, from primary to secondary and to the tertiary. Pupils cared about their own learning and they seldom helped each other. After the handover of the sovereignty of Hong Kong to China in 1997, there was a dramatic change in the education system in Hong Kong. An education blueprint for the 21st century was formulated by the Education Commission of Hong Kong in 2000, focusing on learning for life and learning through life. To follow up the blueprint, the Curriculum Development Council put forward a document on learning to learn in 2001. The document suggested a new curriculum framework which comprised three interconnected components: key learning areas; generic skills; and values and attitudes. Two of the nine generic skills are collaboration and communication. Since then, cooperation in learning among pupils has begun to take up momentum. The case study narrates an interesting **Self-owned Model of School-based Teacher Development** in a school that was struggling to maintain its enrolments until an innovative restructuring of the school and the curriculum, emphasising cooperative learning, ensured the school remained open. It also received a number of awards for its innovation.

The context

Lok Sin Tong Leung Wong Wai Fong Memorial School is located in Hong Kong which is a Special Administrative Region of China. Established in 1983, the school is a government subsidised co-educational primary school. Located in a public housing estate in Tuen Mun, an economically poor satellite town, the school could only attract pupils mainly from families with low socio-economic status. The pupils were diversified in terms of ability, culture and language. Some of them were new immigrants of mainland China, while some were from single-parent families and others were from South Asian countries. The pupils are aged 6–12, studying from primary one to six. With 171 children and 20 teachers in 2008/2009 the school was small compared to most of the others in Hong Kong. The average class size was fewer than 20 pupils.

The school suffered serious enrolment problems in 2008/2009. There were only seven primary one pupils enrolled to the school (the minimum number of primary one pupils required by Hong Kong Education Bureau in 2008/2009 was 21). To avoid shutting down, the school offered a private primary one class. The school could be allowed to offer aided classes only if it would be able to successfully attain the minimum required number of primary one pupils in the 2009/2010 academic year. Heading towards the goal of revival, the school reformed its curriculum with the aim of establishing and maintaining for pupils, a 'happy home away from home' in which pupils, teachers and parents could enjoy a warm, caring family and a place of 'wholeness'. This was achieved by adopting cooperative learning as one of the strategies to foster among pupils a spirit of cooperation and teamwork, cultivate mutual trust and respect among each other, and create a secure and caring environment in the school. The school curriculum reform had proved to be successful as demonstrated by an enrolment figure of 68 pupils in the primary one admission in the 2011/2012 academic year. Since then, the primary one places have been over-subscribed and the school is now making an application for larger premises to meet parents' needs.

Background and rationale for introducing cooperative learning

Since the 2009 report of the Hong Kong Small Class Study recommended learning in cooperative groups as one of the effective learning principles, the Hong Kong government has adopted a policy on small class teaching in its primary schools. As a result, cooperative learning has become popular in the school curriculum. Training programmes are provided by the Education Bureau for teachers to learn how to optimise pupils learning in a small class setting. The programmes aim at enriching teaching in using the six effective teaching principles. They include how to set learning objectives, use extended questioning skills, increase class participation, conduct effective cooperative group work, give informative feedback and use assessment for learning. Over 70% of the primary schools have responded to the policy and used the six effective teaching principles. The use of cooperative learning differs in various schools for various factors. This case study school is fairly unique as it was able to turnaround from closure and become a popular school. A number of things have been done by the school which have acted as a catalyst to bring about a revival. Apart from using cooperative learning, the school has also adopted Invitational Education to create a sense of care and mutual respect, and reconstructed the school facilities to create an innovative learning environment. (See: www.invitationaleducation.net/docs/samples/art_school_transformation_ie_toolkit.pdf.74)

Cooperative learning in practice

A professional development team was set up in the school to coordinate the different kinds of training activities in response to the reformed curriculum. Teachers were encouraged to participate in various modes of professional development activities including seminars, workshops, experience-sharing sessions and different school-based professional development programmes. Furthermore, the school joined the Small Class Teaching Leadership Project organised by the Centre for Development and Research in Small Class Teaching of The Hong Kong Institute of Education. Under the project, a learning circle of schools was set up to provide the teachers with opportunities to take part in lesson observation, mutual sharing and receive support from teachers from the other nine participating leadership schools. The teachers became more sophisticated in their professional development in the areas of cooperative learning, high order thinking, co-planning and co-teaching.

Great importance was placed on enhancing pupils' care to the community and those from the South Asian families. Teams were set up to facilitate the nurture of the caring culture – for example, Big Brother and Big Sister teams, a Community Service team, and Environmental Conservation Ambassadors. By making good use of the advantages of the small class and small school, more than 20 'Caring Groups' were set up, starting from the second term of 2009/2010 school year. Each Caring Group consisted of eight to ten mixed age pupils and was led by a teacher or member of staff. Different kinds of group activities were held once a month on Tuesday evenings. Group mates could discuss the kind of activities they wanted to do with their friends and teacher, for example, playing badminton, catching crabs at the beach, social gatherings at restaurants, etc.

Observation of lessons suggested a high level of learning in cooperation. In one lesson, the teacher used Jigsaw II (Aronson et al., 1978) to teach the pupils how to pronounce 'i / e/ u/' in Putonghua. Having learned the pronunciation properly and quickly, pupils volunteered to help each other. At the end of the lesson, all the pupils were asked to complete an individual quiz in order to test their learning mastery level. The pupils' interview data suggested that they loved to stay in school, especially in the library. They loved to sit on the padded floor, holding their lovely toys while reading. Some mentioned the Story Garden as their favourite place because they enjoyed planting trees and vegetables. Story Garden was an inviting place for them to create their writings and share them with others. The writings from different grade pupils were posted on the walls next to the garden after being laminated by their teachers. The garden had won the award for best school garden in Hong Kong. Moreover, the garden, which was designed in the pattern of the Hong Kong Regional Flag, was frequently made use of to teach the pupils civic education.

Some of the pupils were excited about the after-school activities as they could learn and do creative activities with their peers. All of them loved the Caring Group activities. They were interested to see how their teachers dressed after classes and they loved to spend time with their friends and teacher. At the end of 2009, some pupils went to the northern part of Guangdong in China to serve the people in need. Besides this, the 'Volunteer Service Programme for the Special School Grade One Students' had been awarded 'The Best Ten Volunteer Service Programs' by the Social Welfare Department of Hong Kong.

The school has restructured all classes in primary one to six, and divided pupils into small groups, normally with three to four group mates. These are heterogeneous groups based on their academic performance. Each group consisted of some more able and some less able pupils. In every classroom, desks and chairs of different colours were grouped in fours to arouse pupils' interest and facilitate discussion in groups. In the small class environment, it was easier for the pupils to explore a topic in depth, to work in groups and individually, to reflect on how effectively they had learned and the new skills and knowledge they had developed and constructed. From every lesson observed, the teachers were able to cover a more-in-depth subject content and cater for pupils' diversity more effectively than before.

A school review was conducted by the Education Bureau in 2009. The inspectors visited five times from November to December 2009 to review the quality of the school. The inspectors' judgement was that the school was making good progress, the morale among staff was raised and the school could make good use of external support and resources to benefit the pupils. The school received a number of awards, including for example: the Inviting School Award in 2010; the International Alliance for Invitational Education Caring School Award; and the Best Ten Volunteer Service Programs in 2009. In 2011, after a vigorous review, the school was accepted as an Inventory case by the Centre for Educational Research and Innovation of the Organisation for Economic and Cooperation Development in their Innovative Learning Environments project (see: www.oecd.org/edu/ceri/49751959.pdf). The project aimed to investigate how schools in various countries made use of innovative learning environments to develop in children the competencies needed in the 21st century, such as teamwork, collaboration and capacity for problem-solving.

Next steps

Cooperative learning has been internationally researched and recognised as an effective strategy to enhance pupil learning. This learning together strategy has been widely adopted by Hong Kong teachers, especially in the primary sector, since 2009. It has been demonstrated in this case study that adopting cooperative learning as one of the teaching strategies can bring about many positive outcomes. However, the benefits of cooperative learning are not automatic if teachers do not make changes to their teaching practice. Professional development training should therefore be provided for teachers to help them bring about a change in teaching practices using cooperative group work. To sustain the impact of the professional development training on teachers, continued follow-up and school support are essential. To enhance the effectiveness of school support, Chan (2010) has proposed a model entitled *A Self-owned Model of School-based Teacher Development* to assess the self-efficacy of teachers when trying out cooperative learning in the classroom. The model is made up of six phases in a cycle: (1) setting achievable objectives; (2) participation in sequential workshops; (3) collaborative lesson preparation; (4) specific outcome-based lesson observation; (5) supportive post-lesson conference; and (6) dual reflection.

Case study provided by: Kam Wing Chan, Adjunct Assistant Professor, Department of Curriculum and Instruction; Honorary Advisor, Centre for Excellence in Learning and Teaching, The Education University of Hong Kong

Questions for reflection

1. Discuss the advantages and disadvantages of grouping the pupils in heterogeneous groups based on their academic performance.
2. Consider the benefits of setting up 'Caring Groups' consisting of mixed age pupils.
3. How does the provision of after-school activities that encourage working with peers support this?

Case study 7: Ankur Vidyamandir, India

This case study is of a small inclusive multicultural school in India with pupils that have a wide range of disabilities, along with non-disabled pupils and diversities in religions and castes. It is an enlightening account of how the teachers have developed cooperative learning to embrace diversity and support the wide range of pupils in the school. Inclusive education has been given special importance (a four-credit course in the B.Ed. curriculum) in the latest (2016) teacher education curriculum of India (National Council for Teacher Education, 2016). Cooperative learning is not common in Maharashtra and India, but the teachers do conduct group work. In the past few years constructivism has become an important part of the Indian school and teacher education curriculums. Cooperative learning is known to teacher educators more theoretically, but it is yet to become a routine part of their teaching.

The context

This case study presents the effects of cooperative learning activities conducted in Ankur Vidyamandir, a multicultural inclusive private school situated in the Pune city of the Maharashtra state, India. Maharashtra state is located in the central-west region and Pune is close to Mumbai, the economic capital of India. Pune is also the education hub of India and attracts many migrant communities and people. The majority of the children in Ankur school speak Marathi, but many come from Laman families who are traditionally nomads, now trying to settle. They speak Lamani dialect and are often the first-generation learners. Ankur pupils come from families that speak many different languages at home. Classes one to three, considered in this case study, have an average age range of 7–11 years with extreme diversity in disability, language and socio-economic-educational family background in every class. Out of the total of 54 pupils, 35 suffer varying degrees of severity of disability, both physical and cognitive. There are 38 boys and 16 girls of multiple castes and religions.

Each class is co-educational and has more pupils who have at least four different type of disability; three or more with a cognitive disability and between one and three children who are autistic. Many pupils speak varied home dialects which are different from the language of instruction. Each class has two sections for two instructional mediums: Marathi, the regional language, and English. There is a separate teacher for each section and the two sections share the same room.

Beliefs and attitudes related to disability often create problems in social cohesion and therefore disability becomes an important consideration for intercultural education. The authors believe there is a need for inserting cooperative learning in Indian education to ensure sustainable futures and that this should be emphasised as the most important goal of education at a global level (Agashe, 2005). They note too that inclusive education and cooperative learning are both essential components of sustainable development that are emphasised on the UN 2030 agenda:

> The 2030 Agenda for Sustainable Development is an ambitious, aspirational and universal agenda to wipe out poverty through sustainable development by 2030. When it adopted the new Agenda in September 2015, the international community recognized that education was essential for the success of all 17 of its goals. Ambitions for education are essentially captured in Sustainable Development Goal 4 which aims to 'ensure inclusive and equitable quality education and promote lifelong learning opportunities for all'.
>
> *(UNESCO, 2015)*

Background and rationale for introducing cooperative learning

In India, there is a long history of people of many religions, regions, languages and castes living together. There are 22 recognised languages and hundreds of dialects in India. Hindi is the most common language and in Ankur school the teachers use Hindi orally, as needed, in addition to Marathi and English to help some children learn. The Ankur school also has an ethos of acceptance of diversity and social bonding, kept alive through the variety of inclusive practices in daily routine and activities that bring together the pupils, school staff, parents and community; yet many teachers find it difficult to provide optimal instruction for each pupil in the class. In a typical class, many disabled and linguistically heterogeneous pupils simultaneously require different instruction with individual attention. Cooperative learning is known to maximise disabled pupils' engagement in the learning tasks. Slavin (1995), Katz and Mirenda (2002), Puri and Abraham (2004), Rief and Heimburge (2006) and Rao et al. (2010) all support the use of cooperative learning and teamwork for effective inclusion of disabled pupils. Therefore, in this study teachers' professional development was geared towards cooperative learning in the classroom.

Cooperative learning in practice

Every teacher strongly wished to include every child in the activity and showed concern and care for all of their pupils. But the teachers required professional help to develop the necessary skills. Preparation of the teachers for cooperative learning is crucial for its classroom success (Baloche, 1998; Brody and Davidson, 1998; Ganesan, 2011; Sharan, 2010) and collaborative efforts are valuable in planning and implementation (Jolliffe, 2014). Teachers' communication plays a crucial role in supporting a child's optimal learning (Gillies, 2006) and therefore it was an important topic of facilitation. A cooperative learning expert, Lalita Agashe, visited the school two to three times a week to facilitate the teachers' preparation, planning and supporting the initial implementation of the cooperative learning activities. Later on, for the last four weeks, the actual visits of the expert were reduced to one in ten days, with the system of telephonic discussion every alternate day with the teachers and the supervisor.

The support from the facilitator included group discussions with the teachers using modelling, one-to-one discussions to design and improve the activities to make them relevant to the objective, short, interesting and inclusive. Facilitation also included observing the implementation of cooperative learning and providing suggestions to the teachers where appropriate. In designing the cooperative learning activities, many teachers were helped to identify the specific objectives of the activity clearly and adapt the activity to match individual pupils' difficulties and abilities.

Together, the two class teachers selected and decided the procedure and then shared it with the cooperative learning expert who facilitated the work for the activities. The expert then helped enrich the activity by asking reflective questions to the teacher to facilitate improved learning for every pupil. This kind of one-to-one dialogue and small group conversations between the facilitator and the teachers was valuable for improving the teachers' understanding in order to make suitable adaptations. Adapting the activity for a child with special needs involved making necessary changes in objective, procedure, materials and communication to facilitate the pupils's participation and engagement. As a result, every teacher 'owned' all the activities for their own class. In addition, some teachers used their cell phones for showing language games and stories to the pupils.

The details of the classroom implementation of cooperative learning were as follows:

1. The duration of the cooperative learning activities.

    Generally, a cooperative learning activity required 10 to 15 minutes and was continued for five to ten days. Variety of the cooperative learning activities went on for eight weeks in each classroom.

2. The cooperative learning task and grouping.

    Informal groups of two to five pupils were used flexibly depending upon the task.

    (i) A non-disabled pupil paired with a disabled pupil for peer tutoring and support. For example, a non-disabled girl, Radha, in class one played with Mohan, a boy with delayed development, problematic eyesight and unclear and less speech. Radha held a picture of an animal/bird in her hand saying its name and asked Mohan to find the identical picture from many assorted pictures and hold it in his hand to show her.

(ii) Often the task was differentiated to suit different ability learner-groups. As an example, for mathematics word problems in class three, two non-disabled pupils Dinesh and Shyam were paired together (group one) to design word problems of addition and subtraction and pose these problems to pupils in group two consisting of three girls Meena, Sonal and Smita with intellectual difficulty – autistism, mild cognitive impairment with speech problems and Down's syndrome respectively. They had to identify whether the solution of the word problem lay in addition or subtraction. Group one was asked to design easy problems and help group two to solve if needed.

(iii) Small random groups working and helped by others when needed. For example, in a vocabulary building game, the teacher wrote a word on a chit and kept it in the centre of the small group (three or four). The group members took turns to tell related words.

(iv) A common task for the whole class such as salad decoration. In class four, when the pupils came to know of a peer's birthday, they asked the teacher to provide material to make birthday caps. By helping each other, the pupils prepared beautiful caps the way they had learned earlier, but adding new imaginative ideas to decorate and even improvise using available materials.

3. The subjects covered.

Most of the cooperative learning activities were designed for teaching syllabus-based basic concepts and skills from various subjects including mathematics (shapes, counting and colours using beads, pictures and balls), Marathi and English language (alphabet identification, speaking and conversing, reading pictorial and verbal story, writing), environment education (living and nonliving, water) and co-curricular (making food items, gardening) and cultural activities (celebrating a festival).

The teachers implemented the cooperative learning activities in their classrooms for eight weeks with facilitation from the expert and colleagues. The activities were planned to be continued in the next academic year.

Summary of impact

The pupils and the teachers enjoyed the cooperative learning activities. They were found effective in engaging all pupils with and without disability. The cooperative learning activities helped all the pupils improve their receptiveness and response to the teacher's instruction; participation and engagement; skills of learning individually and in groups; motivation to participate and learn; and improved self-esteem. The non-disabled and some disabled pupils started taking responsibility and initiative for their own learning as well as their peers'. Some pupils showed improved imagination and creativity when they had an opportunity. The teachers improved their understanding and skills of cooperative learning, specifically and in their teaching-learning in general. This change occurred because the pupils received opportunities to express themselves by doing a specific task with peers in an open and accepting environment. There was no pressure in completing a task within a specified time and no harsh comments if a pupil did not respond or responded incorrectly. Pair and small group activities conducted in heterogeneous groups was an empathetic way help build trust. The improved acceptance and encouragement by the peers and the teachers during regularly provided cooperative learning activities has probably made the disabled and non-disabled pupils shed their shyness and hesitation and they were motivated to express themselves openly despite their limited abilities with hearing, speech or other physical and intellectual difficulties.

Some important additional factors that could have added to the effect of the cooperative learning activities are as follows:

1. The decision to make tests suitable to the pupils' ability and way of expression, and removing the emphasis on written test.
2. Yoga and meditation has been a part of the teachers' professional development programme and teachers practise it because they have found it effective. It is helping the teachers manage their stress.
3. Some disabled pupils get help from therapists and they practise yoga.
4. The school presented a musical drama based on a traditional popular epic Ramayana in front of the inmates of an old age home. In this event every pupil of the school played a character in the drama on the stage. The drama practice went on for two weeks just before the cooperative learning activities. It may have helped pupils open up and participate freely in classroom activities too.

On the whole, the use of cooperative learning activities, along with the cooperative learning approach at various levels, was effective for the pupils and the teachers in this multicultural inclusive school in India. It helped develop the 21st century skills of collaboration, communication, critical thinking, problem-solving, learning to learn, ICT and literacy, flexibility, adaptability and initiative, and citizenship. The learning from this case study is valuable and will support carrying on the development of cooperative learning in the next academic year in this school and others. Note: the names of the pupils are changed for confidentiality.

Case study provided by: Lalita Agashe, Facilitator for teachers' professional development including cooperative learning and Madhuri Deshpande, Managing Trustee of COER, Ankur Vidyamandir – Inclusive School

Questions for reflection

1. Consider how cooperative learning enabled pupils to work together, regardless of any disability.
2. Discuss the ways the school has developed an ethos of acceptance of diversity and social bonding.
3. Reflect on the use of yoga and its benefits for pupils at this school.

Case study 8: Using cooperative learning in teaching music in Singapore – when the magic happens

This case study is set in Singapore and is from a self-employed percussion teacher who works with many different ages of children and adults. It illustrates how a teacher working individually can adopt cooperative learning. After undertaking professional learning on cooperative learning by Professor George Jacobs, an expert in this area (Jacobs et al., 2002), this teacher has been inspired by this way of working. He now plans to continue this less traditional approach in his teaching.

The context

Bryan Lucas teaches children aged from 3 to 15 years of age, as well as adults. Bryan works in a variety of settings and is also studying for a Specialist Diploma in Arts Education at the National Institute of Education Nanyang Technological University (NIE NTU). As part of his studies, he attended workshops led by Professor George Jacobs, which featured the use of cooperative learning.

Cooperative learning is receiving increasing attention in Singapore as an alternative to the traditional competitive and individualistic approaches (Tan et al., 2007; Lee et al., 2002). Project work has been implemented in schools in Singapore since 1999. A study by Tan et al. (2007) on the use of the Group Investigation method found that although motivation increased, there were no demonstrable academic benefits. However, a significant finding was that:

> The students were still entrenched in the traditional school and classroom norms. Those norms could be changed only by a relatively extensive school-change project.
>
> *(2007:153)*

More recently, in 2015, the Singapore Ministry of Education has published 21st century competencies (www.moe.gov.sg/education/education-system/21st-century-competencies). These include:

- Civic Literacy, Global Awareness and Cross-Cultural Skills;
- Critical and Inventive Thinking;
- Communication, Collaboration and Information Skills.

Cooperative learning is therefore a powerful medium to support these 21st century competencies.

Background and rationale for introducing cooperative learning

Bryan began teaching music using a more traditional didactic method and found cooperative learning at first by accident, realising that when pupils worked together in groups they were more motivated and engaged. He slowly began to introduce this, helped by attending workshops led by Professor George Jacobs, an education consultant working with schools and universities who has written extensively on cooperative learning (Jacobs et al., 2002; Jacobs 2007; McCafferty et al., 2006). The first time Bryan learned about cooperative learning from Professor Jacobs, he did not immediately make use of it but later tried incorporating cooperative learning into group work and then the 'magic started' and he saw the impact of working in this way. He then began using cooperative learning more often.

Bryan does not believe that using cooperative learning is a matter of different cultures or school systems, but is down to the individual teacher. He felt that once he had decided to use cooperative learning, that was the key: the day he decided to change, everything just happened. So, once Bryan became convinced about cooperative learning, it changed his mind-set about teaching and convinced him that it is far more effective to use interactive cooperative group work than a more traditional approach. That was the major step for him. He has now been using cooperative learning for two years.

Cooperative learning in practice

Bryan finds that some pupils who are not so studious, or those that have particular personalities, find it more difficult to work together. He feels there are two important factors that help:

1. The careful mix of pupils in groups.
2. Use of scaffolding by the teacher and careful explanations. For example, in rhythm creation, it is important to guide the pupils to understand the basic elements, such as using numbers to help the base count.

He works with different pupils all the time who are being introduced to learning percussion and only occasionally does he have the same pupils for two sessions. He finds the benefits of cooperative learning are not only motivational, but also that everyone gets an opportunity to participate.

Using cooperative learning, he has observed considerable change in pupils' attitudes and especially with those who have special needs. For instance, he recalled one pupil who had speech and communication difficulties in a cooperative group work session, learning percussion. The pupil had previously been very quiet but in working cooperatively, he was really enjoying himself. Bryan finds cooperative learning helpful in including such pupils and that their attitudes to each other in groups is different from when they are individuals coming together as a class. When they are all together as a class he finds they can sometimes be quite mean to each other, and if one person makes a negative comment, the others all follow. But when they are in groups they are more caring towards each other.

One strategy Bryan finds useful is something he learned from Professor Jacobs, called the 'attention signal', which works well in a group situation if pupils get a little over enthusiastic and the teacher needs to get their attention. The attention signal works for Bryan when he plays something on an instrument or claps in a specific way and the pupils will reply back.

Bryan does not see substantial differences when working with different ages and feels any differences could be down to teacher inexperience and not adapting and explaining in a way all the children can understand. He would use cooperative learning whatever subject and whatever age, as it is a more effective way of learning.

Next steps

Bryan is very keen to continue with this way of working and hopes to work with Professor Jacobs further. He believes using cooperative learning is mostly down to the teacher's mind-set and that once teachers are convinced and see the impact, or 'magic' of this way of learning and teaching, then they will make use of it.

Case study provided by: Bryan John Lucas, self-employed percussion music teacher

Questions for reflection

1. Consider how this teacher has found that using cooperative learning has changed the attitudes of his pupils.
2. What do you think Bryan means when he states he, *believes using cooperative learning is mostly down to the teacher's mind-set?* Consider the *mind-set* the teacher needs, to implement cooperative learning effectively in their classroom.

Case study 9: Italian primary school, Bologna, Italy: Complex Instruction in practice – challenges and opportunities in a mountain school

The ninth case study is set in a village primary school of 53 pupils in the province of Bologna, Italy. The teacher and researcher used Complex Instruction (CI) as a tool for realising their educational ideal of giving equal opportunities to all pupils, and an effective strategy for developing the intercultural understanding required in a school with a diverse and transient population. See Chapter 3, Phase 1, Establishing a community of learners on page 99 for more information about CI.

This contribution is part of a wider research project (Pescarmona, 2012) which aimed to investigate what it meant for teachers and pupils in heterogeneous classrooms to teach and learn innovatively by experimenting with CI (Cohen et al., 1999). This provides a qualitative evaluation of the process by gathering and analysing data by using an ethnographic methodology. For over two years, participant observation, open interviews and informal conversations were adopted to explore everyday lessons and interactions, and later also during CI practice. This offered a sensitive and holistic understanding of the context and its changes.

The context

This case study examines the implementation of Complex Instruction, which was developed in a primary school placed in a village in the Apennines, in the province of Bologna, Italy, from December 2006 to May 2008. When the experimentation took place, the school included 53 pupils, who were distributed in five classes. Most of the pupils came from neighbouring villages, sometimes rather far away from each other, and belonged to families with a low socio-economic level, limited access to cultural experiences, and an increasing number of recent immigrant families. The number of pupils could change considerably during the school year because of immigration and families moving to and from the city. At the same time, this school was affected by a high level of teacher turnover, which sometimes made the organisation of teaching more difficult. In order to cope with this, the subjects that were perceived more important (mathematics and Italian) were assigned to permanent teachers in each class, while the other subjects were taught by several temporary teachers, resulting in a fragmented timetable.

Thus, geographically isolated and with limited cultural and economic resources, the school was often described by permanent teachers as a 'passing-through school'; a place where both teachers and pupils only stayed for a short while before moving on.

Valeria (a pseudonym) – one of the permanent Italian language teachers – decided to adopt in her 4th grade class of nine-year-old pupils an experimentation with CI. The class consisted of 18 pupils (4 girls and 14 boys). Two of them were Albanian, one Moroccan, one Romanian and two Roma children. This class was described by the school teachers as a 'troubled class' with some disruptive social dynamics which made teaching challenging. But for Valeria, this was a lively class whose diverse members had many abilities and needed to be continuously motivated by various learning proposals.

The reasons for choosing Complex Instruction

The idea of implementing CI in her classes was not new for Valeria. In 2004, she took part in CI teacher training, which was organised by the Intercultural Centre of Bologna, and successfully carried out a short experiment in a 2nd grade class (Augelli et al., 2005). Thus, a few years later, she decided to participate in a research project and carry on developing an original CI teaching unit with a group of primary school teachers in Bologna, and experimenting with using this in her 4th grade class.

Valeria started to be inspired by the principles suggested by Cohen (1994), such as status treatment and multiple abilities approach. According to the teacher, CI was a tool for realising her educational ideal of giving equal opportunities to all pupils, especially to those in such a deprived school context. She believed that the school should work as a means of promoting social justice by offering pupils a wider range of educational activities, thus enabling them to participate in school activities and further on in society. This was a way of overcoming the initial social and economic constraints.

Complex Instruction in practice

Teaching choices and strategies

Implementing CI in this school was not easy at first. Valeria had to mediate time-table, subjects and the use of some school materials with different colleagues, as well as her usual professional way of organising learning activities and relating to the pupils. She also had to manage the pressure of covering an extensive syllabus in a context where she had just a few hours a week in each class, and where she felt a lack of staff support in her educational projects. However, she perceived the experiment with CI as a 'challenge' that she did not want to miss.

Valeria began devoting a lot of time to developing cooperative behaviours in pupils through games. Not only did Valeria make use of Cohen's (1994) skillbuilders, such as 'Broken Circles' and 'Guess my Rule', she invented a new game to engage her pupils: 'The Hidden Picture'. Thanks to the repetition of these games and the class discussions that followed, pupils co-constructed a new set of rules that were displayed on posters. Then, she organised pupils in groups of four to five to look at different learning materials and explore the 'Big Idea' of the new CI unit from four different viewpoints (Art, Italian language, History, Science). *Sapore è sapere?* [*Is tasting learning?*] is the Big idea of the CI interdisciplinary unit that was developed according to pupils' educational level and the Italian National curriculum. This unit examines the role that is played by food in the development of human civilisation. At the end of the session, the groups were required to give a presentation of about five minutes, followed by the teacher's feedback. The teaching unit was repeated three times. Groups were heterogeneously composed by mixing pupils according to their various abilities, level of learning and status perception. Cooperative roles (such as facilitator, reporter, material manager, time-keeper) were assigned, with particular attention to low-status pupils, and rotated at each experiment. In order to adapt CI to her class more effectively, Valeria decided to bring about some variations to Cohen's indications. For example, she allocated extra-time to finish and present the task to the class. She also let pupils use other school spaces, such as the corridor or the gym, to help them work creatively and autonomously. The experimentation with CI and skillbuilders activities were developed one or twice a month during the whole school year.

Dealing with Complex Instruction for pupils

'CI is a real challenge for pupils', explained Valeria. Firstly, pupils had to face a task that was new and 'strange' for them. Secondly, they were required to use abilities that were different from those they were used to, without the teacher's guide. Valeria often reported being worried that some of the pupils may fail or need extra-help.

However, for these pupils the main issue was to create and maintain relationships within the group.

In a context of isolation and lack of a fixed authority and organisation, the peer group had become the 'gravitational point' for staying and learning at school for these pupils. The 4th grade class was characterised by a chaotic atmosphere, where each school event was an opportunity to bargain markers, test answers, stickers or paper-balls with friends. Also, the ability to play football or computer games was a means of bargaining. Being able to carry out these negotiations and forming alliances were at the basis of classroom rules to gain popularity and maintain power positions within the peer group. Therefore, high-status pupils were pupils that were able to successfully manage both school duties and peer requirements, while low-status pupils were those who did not agree, or were not invited, to participate in pupils' exchanges. In both classrooms, there were native Italians as well as foreign-born pupils.

The 4th grade class welcomed CI with excitement and eager anticipation that it would be fun. Sometimes they invented new rules to make the task more interesting for themselves, by pretending to be fantasy characters or redistributing cooperative roles according to the relationships of friendships and power. Instead of engaging in a real discussion, they often preferred just to play about with colours, papers and other unusual, but now available, materials. However, they were also able to adjust their usual way of interacting with the new cooperative norms. This improved their capacity to successfully cope with a complex and multidimensional task, and experiment with new and unforeseen solutions. For example, a group ended up creating a dress with crepe paper for an original tableau, instead of simply drawing a poster. Another group was able to complete the task by miming a story with background music. They started to learn to consider the ideas of each member and achieve a shared solution. Sometimes the 4th grade class dynamics could lead to chaos and they could lose focus, but thanks to the repetition of the experiment and class discussions, some usual peer interactions began to break and new protagonists came to life. In smaller groups, low-status pupils had the opportunity to intervene more frequently and give their contribution. Thus, a lower achiever suggested using a rap rhythm and another realised a perfect staging for his group drama. A shy classmate was even elected the singer of the group, becoming extremely popular among his peers.

Experimenting with CI encouraged pupils to participate and made them more aware of having their voice heard. It developed the conditions for implementing a more democratic dialogue and a fruitful interdependence based on different abilities and expectations, which are at the basis of global citizenship skills. See Pescarmona (2011, 2014) for more information.

Changes in teacher's perspective

This experience is very stimulating for a teacher, reported Valeria at the end of the experience, In a short time you must organise the class, observe groups, give feedback, take notes on pupils' learning competence and interactions and pay attention to low-status pupils. And, finally, you must observe yourself! Implementing CI was a challenge not only for pupils, but also for the teacher. It entailed effort and commitment to overcome school constraints and manage a different way of teaching. However, it also provided the teacher with the opportunity to reflect on her own professional competence. The main point of Valeria's reflection was not so much the pupils' evaluation or a correct application of CI, as her usual way of teaching (Pescarmona, 2017). She stated to be 'more aware' of what she did at school every day. For example, she realised her difficulties in delegating authority or assigning feedback to pupils by using a wide range of abilities. Thus, she was prompted to imagine creative solutions, such as interpreting the syllabus in a more open and interdisciplinary way, or using different materials and resources in order to make everyday tasks more inclusive. A remarkable change was her way of looking at pupils, especially those with low-status. Pupils' status comes out from your teaching method, she explained, and expressed the need to extend CI evaluation criteria into each lesson. CI led Valeria to call into question her usual teaching styles and her previous educational ideas.

However, the experiment with CI had also highlighted the limits of a school context where sharing educational and pedagogical issues with colleagues and organising multidimensional activities was difficult – a situation that could restrict the potential of CI. Whereas she recognised the resistance of her school context to change, she clearly considered herself the main subject of change. She interpreted the CI experience as a 'professional springboard' to innovate her way of teaching.

Final thoughts

Complex Instruction had the potential of being a powerful means of change. It had positive implications in terms of social justice, by providing the teacher with a better understanding of her professional identity, and the pupils with a different way of participating in the learning process. CI revealed itself also as a good tool for managing troubled classrooms. It offered the opportunity of engaging pupils in learning activities in a successful way by breaking the usual norms and social dynamics. This was a particularly worthwhile experience, as in such a remote and deprived school context it is hard to maintain the same high standards of education as in an urban school. Furthermore, CI showed that different ethnic origins of pupils did not influence the learning process, whereas it was affected by the pre-existent school context and the competence that pupils developed through daily interactions.

Case study provided by: Isabella Pescarmona, Lecturer at the University of Turin – teacher trainer/teacher in Secondary School, Department of Philosophy and Educational Sciences, University of Turin, Italy

Questions for reflection

1. Consider how using Complex Instruction can help give equal opportunities to all pupils.
2. How did the use of Complex Instruction change teachers' attitudes and impact on their professional identity?
3. Discuss how cooperative learning has positive implications in terms of social justice.

Case study 10: Charlton Christian College, Australia

The tenth case study is set in New South Wales, Australia, and is from a teacher who has been using cooperative learning for a number of years in different school settings. She believes in developing a democratic classroom environment and this example aptly demonstrates this approach.

The context

Charlton Christian College (for ages 5–18) has approximately 600 pupils. It is situated in Fassifern, in a leafy environment on the western side of Lake Macquarie, south west of the larger city of Newcastle. It is a low fee independent school as it is situated in a lower socio-economic area. The population of Lake Macquarie city is about 205,000, making it the seventh largest regional city in NSW by population. In the past, Lake Macquarie had a history of coal mining, fishing, boat building and manufacturing but these industries no longer exist and unemployment rates are around 5.5%. Lake Macquarie City Council lies within the traditional country of the Awabakal people. Aborigines of the Awabakal nation have lived in the Lake Macquarie area for more than 8,000 years. Julie is currently teaching in the middle school, although she is originally primary (ages 5–12) trained. She currently teaches Years 7, 8 and 10 (ages 12–15) and her class sizes are varied.

Background and rationale for introducing cooperative learning

This independent school aims to create a positive, creative, challenging and caring learning environment (with a Christian ethos). The NSW Education Standards Authority (NESA) is responsible for developing syllabuses to be taught in New South Wales schools, from Kindergarten through to Year 12. All independent schools in NSW are registered by NESA and are educationally and financially accountable to the Board and to the Australian and NSW Governments.

In addition to subject-based content (eight key subjects for pupils aged 5–15), all syllabuses address important contemporary themes and general capabilities as pupils prepare to live and work successfully in the 21st century. These include Australian curriculum cross-curriculum priorities and general capabilities, and other learning across the curriculum areas identified by NESA and as described above in the Australian context.

Developing **personal and social capability** is the key link to cooperative learning. Personal and social capability encompasses pupils' personal/emotional and social/relational dispositions, intelligences, sensibilities and learning. It develops effective life skills for pupils, including understanding and handling themselves, their relationships, learning and work.

The College's motto is 'Equipping for Life' and one of its missions is, 'the provision of a secure, caring, challenging, and positive learning environment for each child' and the fostering of 'a cohesive and supportive . . . community where the teachers, parents and pupils work together for the greater good of each person'. Cooperative learning, therefore, provides a powerful medium to support this motto as well as the school missions and values.

For the past 12 years, Julie has implemented cooperative learning both here and at her previous position in another large independent school, but this time in both primary and middle school settings.

Cooperative learning in practice

Julie was introduced to cooperative learning in her four-year undergraduate teaching degree (BT/BA Primary) and started to use it in the early years of her teaching. She became particularly interested in this approach when she volunteered to work with the author Kate Ferguson-Patrick on a six-month study of professional learning/action research in her third year of teaching. After this involvement, Julie was asked to lead the school in implementing cooperative learning due to her passion and expertise.

She loved the idea of cooperative learning and has used it consistently throughout the 12 years of her teaching career. She adapts it for the age group she is teaching and remembers over the years the impact that cooperative learning has had on particular pupils' self-esteem; especially those with special needs such as those on the autistic spectrum. The ability to complete all roles given (e.g., to be a scribe, a researcher, a reporter) and work together as a team has provided her pupils with life-long learning skills. She acknowledges how important these skills are for all careers. These skills, explicitly taught in Julie's class, are necessary for pupils to learn – they learn by doing. Julie recognises the impact this has on all of her pupils' schooling, that they carry these skills with them once taught, and that in future years they are able to give each other roles in order to complete a group work task successfully.

For the past few years Julie has taught from Year 5 (10–11 years old) up to Year 10 (15–16 years old). In her current context, she commented the pupils are fairly naïve and isolated in their knowledge of world views. She taught a variety of pupils with additional needs including new arrival pupils, a mute pupil, pupils on the autistic spectrum among the learning needs, and supported these pupils through programming for life skills in addition to her usual program, through differentiating her usual learning tasks to accommodate all pupils in her class. She mentioned the importance of ensuring all her pupils have attainable goals that give them the knowledge that they can succeed in her classroom. She now teaches subjects that are more separate in her middle school Year 8 setting, such as English and Geography, and is passionate about integrating these subjects. She used group work in both of these classes. Julie used talking sticks and her Year 8 pupils loved the opportunity to all get a say and offer their opinions: they commented they had never done this before but they loved the opportunity it provided for all of them to have a say. Even the more reticent pupils were encouraged by others in their circle to offer their opinions and felt safe to do so using this cooperative learning strategy. They placed the talking stick in the middle of the circle to offer their point of view or answer about the discussion topic and this was encouraged by both their peers and Julie in her role as a teacher scaffolder during her monitoring of the group.

She currently has a class that is harder to work with; she acknowledged they are not as accepting and they have at times not used the strategies she asked them to (such as the talking sticks/tokens) so she can assess how they were interacting with each other. She accepted that time needed to be spent with her classes to build the class climate and that maybe the timing of these strategies could be affected by the amount of time given to this. Later in the school year she will use talking sticks/ tokens as a strategy that allows each pupils to take a turn and acknowledge that everyone has something to offer. She acknowledged again the importance of her modelling these skills and building this climate for the success of cooperative learning, as well as celebrating the strengths all pupils have in the classroom, so they can also see this and value it in group work situations.

She ensured the groups worked well together by having a journal where they kept records of what they had done, and had individual self-assessment sheets and group work assessment sheets, so that pupils could consider their own contribution to the task, as well as assess how well they had worked together. She asked them to consider whether 'there was a weak link in their chain' and what they could do about this. She asked that they to try to solve this themselves and only became involved if necessary by sitting and listening, and guiding. She stressed the importance of ensuring that the 'weak link' was held accountable and that she wouldn't accept that in group work.

Julie believed in developing a democracy classroom with the key aspects of respect and honesty. Put-downs were not okay in her classroom and she stressed that values and morals were of utmost importance to ensure a successful classroom climate. The pupils were involved in creating the 'classroom guidelines' as a community and this was an ongoing document that could be added to and changed throughout the year. Having a democracy in the classroom environment allowed pupils to own their learning as they voted for the choice given and agreed on the outcome, whether they were in the majority or not. Pupils were the ones who often initiated the ideas for classroom activities and asked her if it could be an option for the next lesson. This decision-making process shows how well they worked as a collaborative learning community.

Julie demonstrated in her classrooms that she had established a democracy class-room by developing democracy knowledge and understanding, using democratic pedagogies and encouraging democratic values. Pupils learned about democracy while experiencing the democratic processes – one that requires collaboration and provides a direct link to cooperative learning as a pedagogy that enables democracy, democratic process and a democratic stance. Pupils recognised their interconnectedness and capacity to work alongside each other in her classroom. Democratic, just and caring classrooms are more likely to have teachers like Julie, who encourage pupils to look at different perspectives as they form their argu-ments and engage in dialogue as they critically analyse and develop interpersonal relationships. Democratic values were taught and pro-social behaviour was encour-aged. By building a democracy stance Julie developed a culture of communication. Democracy classrooms, like Julie's, include the following important key factors: a democratic school culture; teachers with a democracy stance and classrooms with a culture of communication; a community of practice; a rich learning community; inclusive practice; and an environment that emphasises social learning.

This research highlights the benefits of adapting a 'democracy stance' and Chapter 3 will explore in depth how this can be achieved.

Next steps

Julie is frustrated by the increase in administration in the years since she started teaching. She commented there is so much she wants to do as a teacher but she feels like she 'is chasing her tail' with the rise in standardised testing and the constant request for data. She commented on the decreased professionalism of a teacher – that her professional judgement is no longer considered good enough and the frustration of giving pupils a set amount of time to do a test is neither equitable nor fair in allowing you to see what that child can really do in the test context. Despite this, her passion for cooperative learning is still apparent and Julie is going to continue with it. She stated that it works, but it takes a long time. It is not a quick fix and it can take weeks to get pupils trained, but when they do know what they are doing to work in groups successfully, it is so powerful.

Case study provided by: Mrs Julie Oldham, middle school teacher, Charlton Christian College, NSW, Australia

Questions for reflection

1. Discuss the implications of high-stakes testing on the use of pedagogies like cooperative learning.
2. Consider the key features of a democracy classroom and how cooperative learning can add to this type of learning environment.
3. In what ways did the teacher encourage pupil involvement, including self and peer assessment?

Case study 11: Urapunga School, Australia

This case study is also set in Australia but in a remote 100% Indigenous school in the Northern Territory. Kerry, the principal of this small school, demonstrates how 'Visible Learning' (Hattie, 2009) and social emotional learning approaches have developed the pupils' cooperative skills.

The context

Urapunga School is located in the very remote Aboriginal community of Urapunga (Rittarangu), situated between the Roper and Wilton rivers, 320 km south east of Katherine. The community has a population of approximately 100 residents and has a community store, small shire office and an unsealed airstrip. The traditional language is Ngalakaan. Urapunga School is a two-teacher school with generally 30 pupils, ranging from preschool age to Year 6. The pupils are 100% Aboriginal and Kriol is their first language. The school is staffed with a teaching principal, classroom teacher, two assistant teachers, a mobile preschool assistant teacher, cleaner and grounds' person. Urapunga School provides all residents of the community opportunities to engage with the school, including a playgroup, preschool program, schooling for primary aged pupils and regular community events. There is a parent group which meets at least once a term to contribute to school processes, as well as a 'student leadership team' which advises the principal on pupil matters. The school adopted Visible Learning approaches in 2015 to build staff capacity and support pupils to work towards becoming assessment capable learners.

Background and rationale for introducing cooperative learning

The rationale for introducing cooperative learning is based on the school's Visible Learning practice, where pupils set learning achievement goals for themselves, and work within their literacy and numeracy groups towards achieving them using learning intentions and success criteria. The following article describes the Visible Learning approach that the school has embraced: www.teachstarter.com/blog/visible-learning-in-the-classroom. In 2016 they also became a trial site for the Northern Territory Social and Emotional Learning Curriculum, which is very much based on a cooperative learning approach. Social and emotional learning (SEL) is the explicit teaching of the skills needed to identify and manage emotions, set and achieve authentic goals, feel and demonstrate empathy, establish and maintain relationships, and make responsible decisions (CASEL, 2017; McLeod et al., 2017). It is based on the idea that social and emotional skills, like all literacies, can be developed and that these skills promote social and emotional well-being. SEL falls under general capabilities in the Australian Curriculum (ACARA, 2014); specifically, personal and social capability, ethical understanding and intercultural understanding.

Cooperative learning in practice

Literacy and numeracy

Pupils worked together with their teacher and/or Aboriginal assistant teacher to 'unpack' learning intentions and success criteria. Based on their understandings, they set learning goal targets for themselves to achieve for each term. They periodically undertook self and peer progress assessments against the success criteria to check they were on track. For multimodal literacy projects, pupils who were more ICT literate were grouped with younger/less ICT proficient pupils to model practice and share ICT skills. The whole class celebrated individual and group successes. Progress in literacy, particularly reading, had been dramatic since the introduction of goal setting and collaborative guided reading group practices, with 67% of pupils across the school reaching (or exceeding) the reading progress target.

Social and emotional learning curriculum trial

Pupils worked cooperatively through all activities and games in the curriculum, and then reflected both individually and within their groups at the end of each session (one-and-a-half hours weekly). The reflections were usually about which form of collaboration/cooperation a group adopted to achieve a task was most effective and why, and how pupils could apply this approach to other situations, whether they be in a learning or outside of school-based situation. In the context of the social and emotional learning curriculum trial, pupils had gained a wider understanding and vocabulary to talk about social and learning interactions, and were now starting to use the meta-language to support cooperative learning.

Pupils approached assessments a lot more confidently and were genuinely engaged in them as they had an understanding of what they were being assessed on (through the success criteria) and their achievements and progress were displayed in the classroom. Pupils have become a lot more confident in talking about their learning and their achievements, and proudly hosted a pupil-led open day for their families once a term to show and talk about their progress. Pupils had become increasingly independent in setting themselves up for their group learning rotations – everyone had a role and responsibility to fulfil.

Teaching practices had become a lot more inclusive in the school with the introduction of Visible Learning – everyone was on board with 'unpacking' the learning intention and success criteria for each given task or project and ensuring that all language and expectations were understood, which is crucial in an English as a Second Language (ESL) context. The inclusion of learning intentions and success criteria throughout all programming and planning documents had increased teachers' confidence in following the Australian Curriculum and making it more accessible for ESL learners.

Next steps

In her new position this year Kerry hopes to continue coaching teaching staff in cooperative classroom practices using Visible Learning impact coaching methods.

Case study provided by: Kerry Searle, Teaching Principal, Urapunga School, Northern Territory, Australia

Questions for reflection

1. Consider the links between social and emotional learning (SEL) and cooperative learning.
2. Discuss why Visible Learning practices can have an impact on a school like this in an Australian Aboriginal context.
3. In what ways were pupils encouraged to have ownership over their learning?

Conclusion

This chapter has demonstrated how particular contexts in a range of countries include factors that support and inhibit the development of cooperative learning. Despite the government priorities, including the curricula in that country that may include or omit cooperative learning, passionate teachers who have particular beliefs about learning still use this pedagogy. They adapt its use for their own context because they know it is powerful when well implemented: it engages, motivates and supports all learners. They are teachers who believe in preparing their pupils for the 21st century world which should include 21st century learning skills, including that of collaboration. They are teachers and educators who believe in providing all children with the knowledge, skills and attitudes that allow respect and understanding between all groups in society. As these case studies also demonstrate, cooperative learning is a powerful pedagogy that can not only engage and include all children in learning, but also helps in developing the skills required for a globalised world. The next chapter examines in depth how implementing cooperative learning in a carefully staged way is crucial.

Chapter summary

You should now understand:

- cooperative learning can be explored in different ways in different contexts;
- different factors can support and inhibit the development of cooperative learning and this can be related to government priorities and curricula;
- policy contexts in both England and Australia in relation to teaching and learning and cooperative learning;
- case studies can provide concrete examples of cooperative learning in action in different ways.

References

Agashe L. (2005). *Sustainable development and cooperative learning in the formal education system in India.* Paper presented at the International conference on Education for Sustainable Future at Ahmedabad, India, Jan. 18–20.

Ahlquist, S. (2013). *Storyline: Developing communicative competence in English.* Lund: Studentlitteratur.

Aronson, E., Blaney, N., Stephen, C., Sikes, J. & Snapp, M. (1978). *The jigsaw classroom.* Beverley Hills, CA: Sage.

Augelli, A., Gobbo, F., Pescarmona, I. & Traversi, M. (2005). Cooperative learning nelle classi multiculturali. Uno sguardo all'istruzione complessa [Cooperative learning in multicultural societies. An overview of complex instruction]. In: *Quaderni di formazione interculturale [Books of intercultural education].* Bologna: CD/Lei.

Australian Curriculum Assessment and Reporting Authority (ACARA). (2014). *General Capabilities.* Sydney: ACARA. Retrieved from: www.australiancurriculum.edu.au/f-10-curriculum/general-capabilities

Australian Government. (2014). *Review of the Australian curriculum: Final report.* Canberra: Australian Government Department of Education.

Baloche, L. (1998). *The cooperative classroom.* New Jersey: Prentice Hall.

Brand, B., & Triplett, C. (2012). Interdisciplinary curriculum: An abandoned concept? *Teachers and Teaching: Theory and Practice, 18*(3), 381–393.

Brody, C. & Davidson, N. (Eds.) (1998). *Professional development for cooperative learning: Issues and approaches.* Albany, NY: Suny Press.

Chan, K. W. (2010). A self-owned model of school-based teacher development. *Journal of Early Childhood Education, 9*(2), 75–78.

Cohen, E. (1994). *Designing groupwork: Strategies for the heterogeneous classroom.* New York: Teachers College Press.

Cohen, E. G., Lotan, R. A., Scarloss, B. A. & Arellano, A. R. (1999). Complex instruction: Equity in cooperative learning classrooms. *Theory into Practice, 38,* 80–86.

Collaborative for Academic, Social, and Emotional Learning (CASEL) (2017). Retrieved on 28.7.17 from: www.casel.org/impact

DfE (2013). *The National Curriculum in England: Key Stages 1 and 2 framework document.* London: DfE Publications.

Ewing, R. (2012). Competing issues in Australian primary curriculum: Learning from international experiences. *Education 3–13, 40,* 97–111.

Fohlin, N. Moerkerken, A., Westman, L., Wilson, J. (2017). *Grundbok i kooperativt lärande. Vägen till det samarbetande klassrummet (Beginning book on cooperative learning: The way to the collaborative classroom).* Lund: Studentlitteratur.

Galton, M., Hargreaves, L., Comber, C., Wall, D. & Pell, A. (1999). *Inside the primary classroom 20 years on.* London: Routledge.

Ganesan, R. (Ed.) (2011). Cooperative learning. *Experiments in Education, 39*(3), 1.

Gillies, R. (2006). Teachers' and students' verbal behaviours during cooperative and small group learning. *British Journal of Educational Psychology, 76,* 271–287.

Gresnigt, R., Taconis, R., van Keulen, H., Gravemeijer, K., & Baartman, L. (2014). Promoting science and technology in primary education: A review of integrated curricula. *Studies in Science Education, 50*(1), 47–84.

Hattie, J. (2009). *Visible learning.* Abingdon: Routledge.

International Primary Curriculum (IPC). Retrieved on 4.8.17 from: www.greatlearning.com/ipc/

Jacobs, G. M., Power, M. A. & Loh, W. I. (2002). *The teacher's sourcebook for cooperative learning: Practical techniques, basic principles, and frequently asked questions.* Thousand Oaks, CA: Corwin Press.

Jacobs, G. (2007). *Cooperative learning in the language classroom.* Singapore: SEAMEO Regional Language Centre.

Jolliffe, W. (2014). *Interview of Jolliffe W.* IASCE newsletter, *33*(3). Retrieved on 28.4.17 from: https://docs.google.com/a/iasce.net/viewer?a=v&pid=sites&srcid=aWFzY2Uub mV0fGhvbWV8Z3g6MTY0Yzg1NTQwMjY3ZmFkMw

Katz, J. & Mirenda, P. (2002). Including students with developmental disabilities in general education classrooms: Educational benefits. *International Journal of Special Education, 17*(2).

Lee, C. Ng, M. & Phang, R. (2002). Effects of cooperative learning on elementary school children in Singapore. *Asia Pacific Journal of Education, 22*(1), 3–15.

Lingard, B. (2010). Policy borrowing, policy learning: Testing times in Australian schooling. *Critical studies in education, 51*(2), 129–147.

Luke, A. (2010). The Naplan debate: Will the Australian curriculum up the intellectual ante in primary classrooms? *Professional Voice, 8,* 41-47.

McCafferty, S., Jacobs, S. & DeSilva Iddings, A. (2006). *Cooperative learning and second language teaching.* New York: Cambridge University Press.

McLeod, B. D., Sutherland, K. S., Martinez, R. G., Conroy, M. A., Snyder, P. A., & Southam-Gerow, M. A. (2017). Identifying common practice elements to improve social, emotional, and behavioral outcomes of young children in early childhood classrooms. *Prevention Science, 18*(2), 204–213.

Ministerial Council on Education, Employment, Training and Youth Affairs [MCEETYA]. (2008). *Melbourne declaration on educational goals for young Australians,* 1–20. Melbourne: Curriculum Corporation.

Mishra, P., & Kereluik, K. (2011). *What 21st century learning? A review and a synthesis.* Paper presented at the Society for Information Technology & Teacher Education International Conference. Nashville, Tennessee, USA.

National Council for Teacher Education. (2016). *Curriculum framework: Two-year B.Ed. Programme.* New Delhi: India. Retrieved on 4.5.17 from: http://ncte-india.org/Curriculum%20Framework/B.Ed%20Curriculum.pdf

Pescarmona, I. (2011). Creativity and competence in experimenting complex instruction: From the perspective of pupils. *Experiments in Education, XXXIX*(3), 81–90.

Pescarmona, I. (2012). *Innovazione educativa tra entusiasmo e fatica. Un'etnografia dell'apprendimento cooperativo. (Stress and Enthusiasm in Innovating Education. An Ethnography on Cooperative Learning).* Roma: CISU.

Pescarmona, I. (2014). Learning to participate through complex instruction. *Intercultural Education, 25*(3): 187–196.

Pescarmona, I. (2017). Reflectivity-in-action: How complex instruction can work for equity in the classroom. *Journal of Education for Teaching, 43*(3), 328–337.

Polesel, J., Rice, S., & Dulfer, N. (2014). The impact of high-stakes testing on curriculum and pedagogy: A teacher perspective from Australia. *Journal of Education Policy, 29*(5), 640–657.

Puri, M. & Abraham, G. (Eds.) (2004). *Handbook of inclusive education for educators, administrators, and planners.* New Delhi: Sage Publications.

Rao, I., Prahladrao, S. & Pramod, V. (2010). *Moving away from labels.* India: CBR Network (South Esia).

Reay, D., & William, D. (1999). 'I'll be a nothing': Structure, agency and the construction of identity through assessment [1]. *British Educational Research Journal, 25*(3), 343–354.

Rief, S. & Heimburge, J. (2006). *How to reach and teach all children in the inclusive classroom.* (2nd edn). San Francisco: Jossey-Bass.

Sharan, Y. (2010). Cooperative learning for academic and social gains: Valued pedagogy, problematic practice. *European Journal of Education, 45*(2), 300–313.

Slavin, R. E. (1995). *Cooperative learning: Theory, research, and practice,* Boston, MA: Allyn and Bacon.

Tan, G. C. I., Sharan, S. & Lee, K.E.C. (2007). Group investigation: Effects on achievement, motivation, and perceptions of students in Singapore. *Journal of Educational Review, 100*(3), 142–154.

Thompson, G., & Harbaugh, A. G. (2013). A preliminary analysis of teacher perceptions of the effects of NAPLAN on pedagogy and curriculum. *The Australian Educational Researcher, 40*(3), 299–314.

TLRP Research Capacity Building Network (2005). Life beyond the TLRP: Outcomes and recommendations. *Building Research Capacity, 9,* 6–7.

UNESCO (2015). *Education 2030. Incheon declaration and framework for action for the implementation of sustainable development goal 4: Ensure inclusive and equitable quality education and promote lifelong learning opportunities for all.* Retrieved on 28.7.17 from: http://unesdoc.unesco.org/images/0024/002456/245656E.pdf

3

IMPLEMENTING COOPERATIVE LEARNING IN THE CLASSROOM

Learning objectives for this chapter

By reading this chapter you will develop your understanding of:

- the importance of carefully staged implementation of cooperative learning;
- the details of the ten key phases of implementation;
- application of cooperative learning in the classroom;
- different types of cooperative learning.

Introduction

As outlined in the Introduction of this book, in spite of extensive research into the benefits of cooperative learning, there is a lack of its actual use in classrooms worldwide.

Sharan (2010:303) describes this as a, *gap between the promise of cooperative learning and its implementation*. As discussed previously, one of the barriers to implementation is a lack of political will to use this approach. Particularly in the USA and UK this is linked to a focus on external assessment and 'teaching to the test', leading to a tendency to rely on more traditional didactic forms of teaching.

One of the other principal barriers to widespread use of cooperative learning is a lack of effective and sustained professional development for teachers in how to apply this in the classroom. A study by Thanh (2011) found that 60% of teachers did not consider using cooperative learning as they lacked the interest or knowledge. Another study (Nguyen et al., 2006) questioned teachers' knowledge about cooperative learning. This has been confounded by a lack of effective inclusion in teacher education (Jolliffe and Snaith 2017; Hennessey and Dionigi, 2013). One of the underlying reasons, as discussed in Chapter 1, is concerned with teachers' attitudes and beliefs about learning. Without a positive attitude to cooperative learning and a belief that it is worth the effort to put into practice, teachers will be unlikely to use it, or if they do, will easily discard it once they encounter difficulties.

Building on an understanding of cooperative learning, its key principles and a theoretical and research-validated basis, as discussed in Chapter 1, this chapter will set out a detailed phased approach to implementation, with examples of carrying this out in the classroom. While this will support understanding and practice for the individual teacher, it is important to appreciate that to implement this approach, teachers need to work together to support each other. As Häkkinen et al. (2017) argue, there are three aspects to collaborative learning: first, collaborating to learn; second, learning the skills of collaborating; and third, learning to teach by applying collaborative learning approaches. This chapter will examine these and then, in Chapter 4, approaches to professional development will be explored – in particular the importance of sustained school-based continuing professional development (Cordingly et al., 2015; Vries et al., 2013).

Types of cooperative learning

Cooperative learning has spawned a myriad of approaches over the last 50 years, which in itself can cause confusion. The most well-known of these include: Kagan's Structural approach (1994); Student Teams Achievement Division (STAD) (Slavin, 1985); Learning Together (Johnson and Johnson, 1975); Complex Learning (Cohen 1994); Group Investigation (Sharan and Sharan, 1992) and Jigsaw (Aronson, 1978). More details of these can be found in Appendix 2. Understanding the differences between approaches to cooperative learning and when to use them is an important first step.

Johnson, Johnson and Holubec (2013) cite four broad types of cooperative learning: informal cooperative learning, formal cooperative learning, cooperative base groups, and constructive controversy. Understanding the differences between these is a useful starting point.

- Informal cooperative learning involves pupils working together in temporary ad hoc groups or pairs that can last from a few minutes or a whole lesson.
- Formal cooperative learning consists of pupils working together to achieve mutual goals for a specified period which may vary from one lesson to several weeks. The teacher needs to consider the following aspects in applying formal cooperative learning:
  - Making clear the academic objective for the lesson and which cooperative social skill is being reinforced.
  - Decide on how to structure the groups, including the size of the groups, how pupils are assigned to groups, what roles are given and how resources and the classroom are organised.

- o How the academic content will be taught and how the task(s) will be explained, the criteria for success and the behaviours expected.
- o Monitoring the functioning of the groups, intervening where necessary to support collaborative skills and to explain academic content.
- o Evaluate individuals and groups performance against the success criteria and provide opportunities for the groups to reflect and review their progress.

- Cooperative base groups are long-term heterogeneous groups that have stable membership in which pupils help and support one another to make academic progress. They meet regularly and often last for one or more years, providing long-term caring relationships and assistance, for example if a pupil has been absent.
- Constructive controversy is where one person's ideas are different from another's and they have to come to a consensus (Johnson and Johnson 2007). This involves discussion of different standpoints and the advantages or disadvantages of an action, etc. It aims to synthesise a novel solution (i.e. creative and collaborative problem-solving). This form of cooperative learning begins with randomly assigning pupils to heterogeneous groups of (usually) four members and then the group is sub-divided into two, each taking a different position. Each sub-group (a) researches, learns about their assigned position; (b) presents a persuasive case about their position; (c) engages in a discussion in which of the different perspectives; (d) then pairs reverse the perspectives and present a best case for the opposing position; (e) they then agree on a synthesis of the best reasoning from both positions; and (f) reflect on the process so that they may learn from it.

For many teachers beginning with informal cooperative learning, involving spontaneous paired work that can progress from groups of two to four, is the best starting point. Appendix 1 sets out a range of structures that can be used in any lesson to apply informal cooperative learning, such as think/pair/share, where pupils think of a response to an open question, and then they turn to a partner to discuss, followed by pairs sharing responses.

ACTIVITY 3.1: SELECTING APPROPRIATE TYPES OF COOPERATIVE LEARNING

In order to consider what type of cooperative learning to select, review the scenarios below and consider whether informal, formal, base groups or constructive controversy would be most appropriate. Where possible, discuss with colleagues what key factors influence decisions about which type of cooperative learning is most suitable.

(continued)

(continued)

Scenario	Type of cooperative learning	Key factors to consider
In a history lesson, the teacher wants the pupils to check their understanding of a sequence of events that they have been studying.		
In a history lesson, the teacher wants the pupils to consider the various causes of a major event, which they will present in the form of news reports.		
In a history lesson, the teacher wants the pupils to examine two standpoints that provide very different reasons for a conflict.		
Pupils are studying a topic in history for a school term and need to form long-standing relationships to support each other's learning.		

Phases of implementation

Research into the implementation of cooperative learning (Johnson and Johnson, 1996; Gillies, 2003; Brody and Davidson, 1998; Stevahn et al., 2000) indicates that there are three broad aspects in this process: firstly, pre-training preparation, such as examining theoretical perspectives and reconciling personal beliefs about learning; secondly the training itself, which is best undertaken through experiencing cooperative learning; and finally, post-training support to ensure long-term success.

Phase 1: Establishing a community of learners

For cooperative learning to thrive it requires a classroom that is a genuine learning community. This is much more than agreeing a set of rules for group work. It requires establishing a cohesive and a safe environment for pupils to flourish. To do this, teachers need to spend time and effort in establishing the groundwork. Chapter 1 explored how learning about and practising cooperative learning can support a particular classroom ambience, known as a 'democracy stance'. It is useful to revisit the features of a democracy stance. These demonstrate a willingness of pupils and teachers to:

- listen and express thoughts;
- share perspectives;

- ensure genuine dialogue to promote equality, freedom and justice for all;
- develop a climate of trust, respect and tolerance and recognition of equal worth;
- enhance high self-esteem;
- ensure a sense of responsibility by all;
- support risk-taking;
- make informed choices;
- be actively engaged.

Whilst the use of cooperative learning can lead to greater inclusion and democracy in classrooms, Elizabeth Cohen's work on status treatments in classrooms (1994, 2014), (see Chapter 1, pages 34 to 35) shows how beliefs about status characteristics shape the behaviours of individuals in a group. Her approach to cooperative learning, called Complex Instruction, recognises diversity as a learning resource and changes the conditions that influence pupils' participation in the classroom. One of the key ways to achieve this is through assigning roles in groups, and carefully considering the match of roles to pupils in order to utilise their strengths and thereby enhance their status.

Now examine the following case study based on one cited in Gillies (2007) to see how cooperative learning can be inclusive and enhance status.

Case study: Tom's story

Tom was in the second year of high school. He has an intellectual disability that meant that although he could participate in most activities, he had difficulties organising things, such as locating the books he needed for lessons and following instructions. His teachers realised the impact this would have and included him in various cooperative learning groups that they established in their classes.

The result was that Tom found through working in small supportive groups he could take risks with his learning. His peers encouraged him and ensured, that he undertook specific roles. These included helping organise resources, presenting his ideas on a topic through different media, and working with his peers to ensure the project they were working on was completed. This enhanced Tom's self-confidence and increased his status among his peers as they realised he was able to make worthwhile contributions to his group.

Strategies for creating an inclusive classroom ethos

Maslow's well-known hierarchy of needs (1943) provides a clear recipe for how to create a classroom ethos that is inclusive and will be fertile ground for cooperation. Examine Table 3.1 and where possible discuss this with a colleague, adding further ways to support each need in the classroom.

TABLE 3.1 Meeting Maslow's hierarchy of needs through cooperative learning

Needs	How to support in the classroom
1. Biological and physiological (food, drink, shelter, warmth, sleep, etc.)	Knowing the background of the pupils and seeking help from others in school where there may be concerns. Providing drinking water in the classroom, and considering nutrition through breakfast clubs, school lunches, etc.
2. Safety (protection, security, law, stability, etc.)	Children need to feel safe to learn. Again, knowledge about children and their background can be crucial, seeking appropriate help from others where necessary.
3. Belongingness and emotional (being part of a family, group, having positive relationships and friends)	Children (as do adults) need to feel they belong – in this case, to the school and the class in particular.
4. Esteem (achievement, status, responsibility)	Well implemented cooperative learning can ensure a high status for all and celebrate pupil diversity. This in turn will require a sense of responsibility to the class or group and support improved achievement.
5. Self-actualisation (personal growth and fulfilment)	Self-actualisation is supported by improving self-esteem and relationships; leading to greater sense of personal fulfilment.

Getting to know each other

One of the most important first steps in building an inclusive classroom ethos is ensuring that pupils have opportunities to get to know each other. Too often teachers assume that because pupils spend a number of years in a school or a class, they will know each other but apart from a few friends, this is often not the case. It is also vital that the teacher gets to know the pupils well early in the school year. One important part of this is knowing each other's names. **The name game** is one way of doing this.

The name game

The aim of this activity is for the children to explain the history of their name to a partner. It requires the following steps:

1. The teacher models what is needed.

    This usually includes the history of the name if known, who gave the person the name and any other information about the name. For example, the teacher's first name is Wendy. She explains it was given to her by her mother who loved the story of Peter Pan written by J. M. Barrie. Barrie's friend called him 'fwendly' instead of 'friendly' because she could not pronounce the letter 'r' and out of this Barrie devised the name 'Wendy' for the story of Peter Pan and Wendy.

2. The teacher asks the pupils to work with a partner and to carry out a three-step interview where each child in turn explains what they know about their name and how they got it, while their partner listens carefully.

3. The teacher first ensures that everyone has had a chance to talk to their partner then asks the pairs to form a four by working with another pair (or a trio or five depending on the numbers of pupils in the class). The children then have to explain to the group about their partner's name.

4. The teacher monitors to ensure everyone has taken part and then asks for any groups who would like to tell the class about an unusual name or how they got the name.

This activity helps not only in remembering and knowing names but ensures full participation and begins forming positive relationships. For other games that help promote multi-culturalism and diversity see: http://wilderdom.com/games/MulticulturalExperientialActivities.html

Celebrating diversity

It is important to realise that valuing diversity does not mean ignoring difference and treating everyone the same, but instead seeking out differences and using it to highlight richness in the classroom. Having pupils from different faiths or cultures, for example, who may speak other languages, can be beneficial to enrich understanding of different ways of life. The teacher is the most powerful role model here, through what they do and say, and through providing opportunities for differences to be recognised and appreciated. This demonstrates that each pupil is valued and the classroom is a much more interesting place because of this diversity. See the following case study for one activity carried out by a teacher to highlight this. Anna, a teacher in England, developed this activity from *Puzzle Pieces*, by Diane Senn and Gwen M. Sitsch (2001). She was working with pupils aged 6–7 years.

Case study: M&M sweets – what is the best part?

> *Anna prepared two shoe-boxes the same size and wrapped one with pretty wrapping paper and a nice ribbon, and the other one with newspaper and string. Inside the box with the pretty wrapping, she put rocks and inside the box with the newspaper, she put M&Ms (coloured sweets).*
>
> *Anna introduced the gifts to the class and asked them if it was their birthday, which would they choose and why. She found the pupils always wanted to pick the box with the pretty wrapping paper. After they have attempted to guess what is in the boxes, she opened the box with the pretty paper and showed them the rocks inside.*

All the pupils now said they had changed their mind about which box. She then opened the box wrapped in newspaper and showed them the M&M sweets. She talked with the class about the differences and that although the box which was wrapped nicely was not so nice on the inside and vice versa with the other box. This led to discussion about how people look on the outside and whether, for instance, if they have nice trendy clothes they are better people. The point is that we need to get to know people to find out.

After this discussion, Anna passes out the different coloured M&Ms for everyone to taste and asks them what is the best part. In unison, the class says: 'THE CHOCOLATE!' She explains that the colour does not matter and further demonstrates this by having a pupil come up in front of the class, close their eyes, and taste an M&M. They need to try to guess what colour it is, but of course they can't tell. The key point is that people are like M&Ms; it doesn't matter what we look like on the outside, it's what's on the inside that counts. We should choose our friends by the way they act and treat others, not by how they look.

Questions for reflection

- Consider how useful this type of activity is in demonstrating diversity.
- How could you adapt it for your context?
- How important is the discussion that follows this?

Building class identity

Many of the activities that support class identity also refer to team identity and team-building, as detailed below. Important aspects include setting up regular class meetings and/or having circle discussions or circle time. In order to ensure a democratic classroom, regular scheduled class meetings are an important feature. For older pupils, they can take on the role of chair for the meetings. Agendas could be similar each time and include:

1. Announcements.
2. Solving problems.
3. Ways of improving the class.
4. Planning events.
5. Celebrating achievements.

The use of a class feedback box where pupils can fill in cards (see Figure 3.1), which are then placed anonymously in the box, can also then be used to form items for discussion at the class meetings. It is important that any decisions are reached democratically, e.g. using a voting system so that pupils see they have a genuine input into the running of the class. This helps in building the class identity and ethos.

Class Feedback

1. What do you think is good about this class?

2. Is there something that could be better?

3. How could learning be improved in this class?

4. Do you have any other comments?

FIGURE 3.1   Class feedback

Activities to support cohesion

There are a number of games and activities that will support class cohesion and could be ideal for the start of a school year or term. A few examples are given below. For a further range of resources for building cohesion see: www.abc.net. au/btn/story/s4102605.htm.

1. Broken circles

    This game was developed by Nancy and Ted Graves (Graves and Graves, 1985) and is based on the Broken Squares game invented by Bavelas (1973). The class is divided into groups of three to six pupils. Each pupil is given an envelope with different pieces of the circle. The goal is for each pupil to put together a complete circle. In order for this goal to be reached, there must be some exchange of pieces. Group members are not allowed to talk or to take pieces from someone else's envelope. They are allowed only to give away their pieces (one at a time). The class are told the task is not finished until each of them has a completed circle. They raise their hands when everyone has finished. You can find instructions and templates for the circles at: https:// web.stanford.edu/class/ed284/csb/Broken/BC&Stext.doc

2. Cooperation clubs

    The aim of this activity is to work together in teams to come up with a club. It can be adapted for different ages but is more suitable for ages 7–12. Each club needs to have:

    1. A club name.
    2. A purpose for the club, e.g. a chess club.
    3. A president.
    4. A secret password.
    5. A logo.

    It is important to allow pupils to resolve this themselves and only intervene if they request help. Provide a specified amount of time and as you monitor the groups, remind them of the time left. Once the pupils have all completed the task they present their club to the rest of the class. You can do a similar activity where pupils create a country.

It is important to reflect on how they carried out the task. Discuss what behaviours helped the group work effectively, and what behaviours were not as productive. Some discussion that supports this includes:

- How did you make decisions as a group?
- Did one person take over?
- Did any members sit back and let others do the work?
- What could have helped your group work better together?

3. The cooperative tray

The purpose of this is for pupils to recognise that you are able to accomplish more as a team than you are alone.

Preparation:

You will need a tray and about 15 random items.

Mount the items onto the tray securely using mounting tape, tack or glue. Use a type of cloth to cover your tray.

Activity:

You begin the lesson by pretending that it is a test. Each pupil has a pencil and paper and they are told they it is important and there should be no talking or cheating. They have to write numbers 1–15 on the paper (or however many items you have). Explain that it is an individual memory test and each child should cover their paper so no one else can see.

You then walk around the room showing each table the items on the tray and say no one should start writing until you say 'Go'. Once you have shown the items to everyone, cover the tray and tell the pupils to begin writing. Usually pupils remember about six to eight items from the tray. Explain that this is about what you expected. Now explain that you want to see how well they will do as a team. Allow pupils to work with a partner, or their group, to see if they can get all 15 items. They usually remember more items, but not all 15. Then explain that they will work as a whole class to see if they can remember all the items, taking different contributions from the teams. The whole class can easily remember them all.

Following this, pupils reflect in pairs and teams on the activity and the benefits of working as a team and a whole class.

4. Friendship stories and parables

Reading stories such as *How to lose all your friends* by Nancy Carlson (1997), suitable for ages 6–8 years, can be useful in identifying first how not to make friends. This can be followed by discussion about being a good friend and creating a class book about friends, where the teacher models an example and then the children are asked to work in pairs to write about being a good friend. These are then collected into a class book to be illustrated.

Parables that contain a message or fables that contain a moral can also be useful. One example is the 'Goose story' which is often used to encourage children to think about the value of cooperating. You can read the story (see below) or watch a short video, such as: www.youtube.com/watch?v=HGY9i8iJu94.

It is important to follow up and consider with the pupils what we can learn from the geese.

Goose story

In autumn when you see geese heading south for the winter, flying in a 'V' formation, think about why they do this.

As each bird flaps its wings, it creates uplift for the bird immediately following. By flying together in a V formation, the whole flock increases its flying range much more than if each bird flew on its own.

When a goose falls out of formation, it suddenly feels the drag and struggle of trying to fly alone and quickly gets back into formation to take advantage of the lifting power of the bird in front.

When the head goose gets tired, it goes back and another goose takes the lead and flies at the point of the V.

To provide encouragement, the geese honk to encourage those in the front to keep up their speed.

When a goose gets sick or is wounded and falls out of formation, two other geese fall out with that goose and follow it down to lend help and protection. They stay with that fallen goose until it is able to fly or until it dies, and only then do they launch out on their own or with another formation to catch up with their group.

If we have the sense of a goose, we will stand by each other like that.

Follow-up questions

How did the geese support each other?

Could the same apply to people?

How does it feel to know that you will get help if you are difficulty?

You will also find further helpful resources for developing harmony in the classroom at: www.harmony.gov.au/resources.

KEY LEARNING POINTS

Phase 1 has examined how to establish a community of learners in the classroom. Some of the key factors are:

- Ensure that as the teacher you model valuing diversity in the classroom and encourage the children to do the same.
- Get to know the children well and ensure they get to know each other. Reinforce this by using activities that encourage maximum participation with different partners so they work with as many class members as possible.
- Help to create a democratic classroom that encourages pupil participation and decision-making, using class meetings.
- Spend time, particularly at the beginning of the school year, in creating class cohesion using different activities such as some of those detailed above.

The next section looks at how you can support cooperation through the management of the classroom.

Phase 2: Classroom management and developing classroom norms of behaviour

Before beginning to make use of cooperative learning in the classroom it is important for teachers to understand how to manage pupils positively and become a facilitator of learning, or in the words of a well-known saying, 'the teacher becomes a guide on the side and not a sage on the stage'. This phase looks at methods to enable cooperative group work to take place, and avoid encountering the many difficulties that teachers may experience in working in this way and devolving the responsibility for the learning to pupils. There are a number of steps (set out below) that can support teachers in organising the classroom.

1. Decide on the group size. Some tasks may only require pairs with pairs becoming fours (or fives for odd numbers of pupils) where appropriate. Then decide how the pupils will be grouped. There are three major ways of assigning pupils to groups:

    1. Random selection (see Figure 3.2).
    2. Pupil selection – this is often problematic when pupils choose their groups, usually by friendship, and can reinforce cliques in the class. However, some teenagers prefer this and it may be useful in some circumstances.
    3. Teacher selection – often more appropriate in trying to ensure heterogeneous groups that are appropriately balanced. It is particularly important for long-term groups.

Strategy	How to use it
Line-ups/count offs	Pupils line up in order with a given criteria (e.g. height, or according to how confident they are about a topic). The line is then segmented into groups of say 4.
Number off	Pupils are numbered according to the size of the groups, e.g. the teacher goes around the room numbering each pupil 1 to 4. Then all the 1s go together and the 2s, 3s and 4s.
Lucky dip	Pupils pick from a bag of objects that can be grouped, such as coloured sweets, buttons, blocks or straws. They then form groups with pupils with the same colour, etc.
Group cards	Pupils are all given cards with different words, numbers or symbols on. They have to match up letters to form a key word, or link paragraphs from a text, match up a question and answer, link parts of a mathematical equation.
Animal noises (A useful strategy for younger pupils)	Pupils are given a small picture of an animal (e.g. dog, cat, pig, cow). They walk around the room making the animal sound (e.g. oink, oink) looking for their team mates making the same noise.

FIGURE 3.2 Grouping pupils by random selection

There are also useful ICT tools to help you create random teams, or to make teams based on skills and interests or to record teams' progress. See http://teamup.aalto.fi.

2. Set time limits

Estimate how long the task will take and make the time limit clear to the class. Using a counter that is displayed on the whiteboard or screen is particularly useful.

3. Arrange the classroom

In order for pupils to work together they need to preferably be seated 'eye-to-eye' and 'knee-to-knee', in other words facing each other. For groups of four you may want to consider 'shoulder partners' – that is two pupils sitting next to each other, with 'face partners' being the opposite pair. You may need to move the chairs and tables during a lesson for this, and getting the class to practise moving quietly and quickly to different configurations is useful. Sometimes a horseshoe or hollow square arrangement may be effective and it is possible in a very short time to rearrange the classroom with the pupils' help. Ideally, groups should be separated to avoid distraction but in some classrooms, space is an issue. Watch the following short video to see one example of a very crowded classroom:

www.youtube.com/watch?v=4y2IaAC5vj4

To see how this was resolved, involving some reconfiguring of the furniture, see the resulting solution:

www.youtube.com/watch?v=Ml17ynz8FG4

4. Use management signals

The use of signals avoids the need for the teacher to have to raise their voice to maintain a calm and pleasant atmosphere. One important signal to develop is **zero noise**, a signal that asks for silence by all pupils and for their attention. Commonly, a raised hand is used and pupils copy by raising their hands. It acts like a ripple around the classroom in everyone stopping and being quiet. Other signals for zero noise are the use of musical instruments, or bells, or hand claps in a particular rhythm. Teachers need to use what works for them.

Another useful signal is **1-2-3 move**. This is for when pupils have to move to groups, or for other classroom movement. The teacher raises one finger, signaling one (and says nothing, modelling silence), and the pupils start the agreed sequence. For example, on 1, pupils put their books in a neat pile. The teacher signals 2 with two fingers and the pupils move to the second step, e.g. standing behind their chairs. Finally, the teacher raises three fingers and the pupils move silently to the allotted place in the classroom.

5. Monitor the pupils

One aspect of this is to check on the **noise levels** in the classroom, as with groups busy talking it can become noisy. One of the skills (discussed in Phase 4) is using quiet voices so that only a partner or group member can hear. Teachers may want to use a variety of methods to encourage correct noise levels, some have 'noise monitors' on the wall in the form of a dial which they turn down, to remind the pupils. There are also different apps such as 'Too Noisy' (http://toonoisyapp.com).

Another important aspect is the monitoring of the groups while they are working. Using **three sweeps** works particularly well for this. This works as follows:

Sweep 1: As soon as the pupils begin their group work, walk around and ask a few pairs or groups to check they know what they are doing. If several do not, it is best to stop the whole class and explain the task again and say that you did not make it clear.

Sweep 2: This is about halfway through the task to check on progress and intervene where necessary. Ensure that plenty of reinforcement and praise is given for pupils working well together.

Sweep 3: This is towards the end of the allotted time to remind pupils on what they need to have accomplished or what they need to report and that time is almost up.

6. Reporting

One of the issues of pupils working together in groups is how they report back at the end of the lesson. If you ask each group in turn it is time-consuming and can become repetitive, so varying the reporting is very useful. There are a number of structures that can be used (see Appendix 2 for details), for example:

Two stay and two stray, where two pupils from the group go to another group to see how they have completed the task and then report back to their own group.

Roam the room, where pupils move in an orderly fashion from table to table to see the different products.

Doughnut (or inside-outside circle), where half the class forms a circle facing outwards and the other half forms an outer circle facing the other circle. The teacher asks the pupils from the inside circle to talk to the person opposite about what they learned from the lesson, or a significant aspect. The person on the outside has to recall this and on a signal from the teacher the outside circle rotates an allotted number of places. The person on the outside now tells their new partner opposite what their previous partner learned or told them.

Post and praise, where pupils 'post' a finished product from a lesson around the room. Groups move around the room in an orderly fashion and write one positive comment on each, using a sticky note or feedback sheet.

7. Evaluate and reflect

Teachers and pupils need to evaluate progress of how the groups are working and how well they completed the task. It is important to allow groups time to do this in a lesson as this is a key part of developing the skills of working cooperatively. Setting cooperative objectives for the lesson, as well as academic ones, can then form the focus for the reflection. Reflection involves three aspects:

1. Evaluating how well they completed the task and worked together.
2. Analysing what they did and what helped or hindered the group.
3. Setting goals that will help the group function better.

Some reflective questions for them to consider can be helpful, such as:

- What went well in your group today?
- Did everyone participate?
- How well did everyone carry out their roles?
- What do we need to do differently next time?

Pupils need support to be able to reflect, as initially they will usually say it all went well. They need to be encouraged to make specific comments such as, 'our group did not finish the task as we talked too much about other things'. If any rewards are given for good cooperation, it is important that rewards such as team points should be given to groups or pairs and never to individuals. Rewarding individuals will counter the benefits of working as a team.

Classroom norms of behaviour

Agreeing the expectations, or norms of behaviour, in a cooperative classroom is also important. Some of this will link to teaching the skills of cooperating in Phase 4.

Norms are shared expectations of how individuals should behave, think and feel. They are not the same as rules, which are often created by teachers to manage pupils. It is important for the pupils to develop these norms through discussion and the following steps can be used:

- The teacher explains what a norm or shared expectation is and gives examples such as 'be kind to others' and 'keep your hands and feet to yourself', explaining that it is better to be positive with them.
- The pupils then have time to work in pairs or groups to list those they think are important.
- Lists are then shared and reviewed, in order to agree those that are essential, such as 'everyone participates', and 'help one another', etc.
- This is regularly discussed at class meetings.

KEY LEARNING POINTS:

Phase 2 has examined classroom management for cooperative learning and developing norms of behaviour. The key aspects include:

- Deciding on the group size and the method of selection.
- Setting time limits for activities.
- Arranging the classroom so pupils can be 'eye-to-eye' and 'knee-to-knee' to help in facilitating working together.
- Using signals to aid the smooth and calm working environment, such as zero noise and 1-2-3 move.
- Monitoring the pupils working, for example using 'three sweeps'.
- Considering methods for groups to report back following activities.
- Making time for reflection as this is a key part of developing the skills of working cooperatively.
- Agreeing the expectations, or norms of behaviour for working together cooperatively.

Phase 3: Team-building

Putting pupils in groups does not automatically result in cohesive teams. When using formal or base groups it is essential to spend some time team-building. It is also much easier to create effective teams if some time has been spent on creating a cohesive class community using the strategies discussed in Phase 1. There are some key steps in team-building and some have similarities with the class cohesion activities.

1. Ensure that the team knows each other and have some 'getting to know you' activities and ice-breakers. Examples of these are listed here (see Appendix 1 for details):

    - Two truths and a lie where each pupil has to tell two true things about themselves and one untrue (e.g. my brother is allergic to horses, I have a pet tarantula, and my dog is bigger than a wolf). The group has to work on which is the lie. Alternatively, the group can be given three things on a card and they decide together which of them is the lie.
    - Three-step interview such as 'sell your house' where pupils describe their house to a partner but are allowed to exaggerate to make it more interesting. The partner listens carefully and later, working with another pair, the partner 'sells' the house to the group.
    - Tell their 'scar story' to a partner where they explain how they got a scar. Members of a team share and decide on who has the most unusual story.

2. Create a team identity

    - Windows, or this is sometimes called 'One and All' (see Appendix 1). First a box is drawn in the centre of a piece of A4 paper. Secondly, a corner of the box is connected to the outside corner of the paper. Third, corners are connected to each corner of the paper to create a 'window'. Each outside section is numbered 1 to 4 with a blank in the middle. In turn, pupils have to write down something about themselves, such as what they particularly like to eat, a hobby or a favourite sport. When each member of the group has recorded something, they decide what they have in common and this is used to decide on the team name which is recorded in the middle segment. Once a team name has been decided, the team agrees a banner or logo and a team 'cheer' to celebrate their achievements.
    - Squiggle art. Here the team is given one piece of A3 paper. Each pupil draws one line on the paper and then passes the paper to the person on their right. The paper goes around to everyone and then continues until they are asked to stop with each person building on what others have drawn to create a picture. These are shared with the class and can be used to help create the team name.

3. Build trust. A range of games can be used for this including:

    - Mirror-mirror – here, pairs of children stand facing each other about half a metre apart. One pupil is the actor and the other is the mirror image. The pupils are given some written scenarios which only the actor can see and then they have to enact it. Their partner can only follow the actions and there is no speaking. After each scenario, partners swap. Scenarios could include:

- o playing football/netball etc;
- o brushing teeth/hair;
- o writing in class;
- o shouting for help as the building is on fire.

4. Respect one another's views

    This is where teams need to come to a consensus for various scenarios.

    - Predicaments. Using a list of predicaments which can be printed on cards, pupils in a group take turns to read out a predicament and discuss an answer. They can write down possible answers, but must agree on one for each within a given time limit. Predicaments can include:

        - o Your house is on fire and you only have time to save five things. What are they?
        - o You are accused of stealing some money by the teacher. You did not do it but you know who did. What do you do?
        - o Someone is spreading lies about you on social media. What do you do?
        - o Your friend left her favourite toy at your house. You really want this toy. Do you keep it and not tell her?

    - Survival activities are another good way to help build teams. You can find a number of these scenarios on the internet such as survival in the desert or on the moon, or after a disaster such as an earthquake (see: http://wilderdom.com/games/descriptions/SurvivalScenarios.html). In many of these, teams have to rank or choose certain items that are necessary. Teams need to discuss and agree on these within a time limit. Debriefing afterwards should look at how decisions were made, whether everyone's views were considered, and if they found disagreement, how this was resolved.

5. Team projects

    Setting a project for the group to solve is a good way of team-building. Examples include:

    - Rectangles, where pupils work in teams to find as many rectangles as they can in a three by three rectangle, or a four by four rectangle (see Figure 3.3). They can begin by working with a partner and then compare with others in their group and agree. They need to consider what strategies they used and also what they did well as a group and what they could do even better.
    - Analysing a poem, or extract of text, together and agreeing the answers to a set of questions. For example, using *Jabberwocky* by Lewis Carroll, pupils are given a copy of the poem, or it is displayed on the whiteboard. Pupils are asked to write at least three different answers to questions and come to a consensus as to the best possible answers. They must work cooperatively to provide one set of answers from the group and everyone must agree and be able to explain.

FIGURE 3.3 How many rectangles can you find?

KEY LEARNING POINTS

Phase 3 has examined ways of team-building in order to help create cohesive teams. Key points include:

- Ensure that the team knows each other and have some 'getting to know you' activities and ice-breakers.
- Create a team identity using a range of activities.
- Build trust using various games and activities.
- Respect one another's views using activities which require coming to a consensus.
- Set team projects for the group to solve to help build the team.

Phase 4: Teaching the social skills

A common assumption is that pupils, particularly as they reach a certain age, possess the necessary interpersonal and teamwork skills for them to be able to work together. However, it is important to realise that we are not born cooperative and we need to learn to act in this way. One of the common causes for groups not working well together is a lack of skills to do this. This is often because in the past they have been expected to work individually and been directed by the teacher. There are two aspects to developing the necessary skills; one is developing the *will* for pupils to work together – in other words, they want to do it as they see it is better way of working. The other aspect is the *skill* or *skills*, which need to be explicitly taught. For many teachers, time spent at the beginning of the school year, or term, is an appropriate time to focus on this, with reinforcement during citizenship or other similar types of lessons. Time invested in this is well rewarded, but frequent revisiting during cooperative group work is also crucial.

It is important first to consider what skills are needed and to note there are two types: **task skills** and **working relationship skills**. Task skills are focused on the content of the task and include:

1. Following instructions.
2. Staying on task.

3. Generating and elaborating on ideas.
4. Managing time successfully.
5. Planning and reviewing progress.

Working relationship skills are focused on the relationships within the group and include:

1. Everyone participating.
2. Helping and encouraging each other.
3. Reaching agreement.
4. Showing appreciation.

Both types of skills are important for groups to function effectively. David and Roger Johnson (1999) propose that there are four levels of cooperative skills:

1. Forming – the basic skills needed to establish the group.
2. Functioning – the skills needed for managing the group's activities to complete the task and maintain good relationships.
3. Formulating – the skills needed to build a deeper understanding of the material being studied.
4. Fermenting – thinking and cooperative skills needed to function at a high level.

Jolliffe (2007:74) developed a 'pupil-friendly' version of a progression of skills into a four-stage rocket (see Figure 1.2, The four-stage rocket of cooperative learning skills, on page 31):

Stage 1 – 'Be ready' including skills of active listening, everyone participating, use quiet voices, no 'put downs', stay with group on task and move silently to groups.

Stage 2 – 'Keep steady', including skills of complete the task, give and ask for help, explain and say why, show appreciation, work together as a team.

Stage 3 – 'Get going', including skills of plan, do, review, reach agreement, summarise, use group roles.

Stage 4 – 'Blast off!' including skills of asking challenging questions, put ideas together, reflect on progress and set goals.

A helpful progression in skills by McGrath and Noble (1993:70), delineates the skills required, moving from starting group work to basic and more advanced skills:
Starting out

- Eye contact
- Smiling

- Body posture
- Tone of voice
- Personal space

Basic group skills

- Sharing and taking turns
- Including others
- Being positive
- Expressing your opinion
- Listening and asking good questions

Advanced group skills

- Respecting other people's ideas and opinions
- Negotiating
- Mediating when others can't agree
- Suggesting and persuading instead of bossing

Group work skills

- Making decisions in a group
- Managing time
- Summarising
- Clarifying

Group learning and thinking skills

- Brainstorming
- Challenging assumptions
- Building on other people's ideas

You may find it helpful to compare these different lists of skills and then create one that is relevant to your context. The next section looks at how to teach these explicitly.

Stages in teaching the skills

The necessary skills need to be taught specifically in stages as follows:

1. Establish the need for the skill.
   The best way to do this is to carry out a role-play that demonstrates why the skill is needed. For example, for active listening, role-play poor active listening using either two adults (such as the teacher and a teaching assistant),

Looks Like	Sounds Like	Feels Like

FIGURE 3.4 Double T Chart

or two pupils who have been briefed first, where one speaks and the other behaves badly, e.g. not giving eye contact, fidgeting, looking at their mobile phone, etc. Pupils soon see what is wrong with this and it is important to follow this by discussing what this should look like, and for younger pupils, role-playing good active listening.

2. Define the skill.

The next step is to define what the skills looks like. The use of a T chart is a useful way to do this. Draw a large T on the board with one side of the T marked 'sounds like' and the other 'looks like'. Ask the class to work in pairs or groups to draw up a list of what the skill should sound like and look like. A double T chart can be used with older pupils which also includes 'feels like' (see Figure 3.4). This chart can then be displayed to form a reminder in the classroom while the skill is practised.

3. Guided Practice

Once the skill has been clearly defined, provide opportunities for pupils to practise it with feedback. It is useful to have a skill that is the focus for a week that is carefully monitored with feedback provided on progress. Ensure that plenty of encouragement is given, provide time for reflection on the skill being practised and set goals for future lessons.

4. Generalised application of the skill is the final stage, with revisiting of the key aspects where necessary.

Conflict resolution

An inevitable part of working with others is that at some point conflict will arise and one of the important skills is learning how to deal with conflict. Making use of class meetings to discuss conflict and how to resolve it is also useful. However, avoid using public situations to cite particular pupils as this could be destructive.

Procedures for conflict resolution

The two important aspects to resolving conflict are: first, being able to stop and calm down; and second being able to see another person's point of view. Pupils often do not know how to deal with disagreements. They may engage in personal attacks or 'put downs', get up and walk away, or even become physically abusive. To ensure successful group work, strategies are needed. It is also important to realise that some minor disagreements can be quickly resolved and when using roles in groups, having a participation checker, for example, as the person who checks that someone's views are being taken into account can help avoid escalation. However, sometimes a more serious conflict will occur and this is where the use of 'I feel' statements is a good way to defuse the situation. Here, the pupil changes any blaming statements into 'I feel' statements in which they express honestly how they feel in response to the other's behaviour. For example, a pupil might say, 'I feel like no one wants to listen to me or work with me when you laugh at my ideas'. This provides an opportunity for the other person to explain the basis for the negative statement and the situation is defused.

Another way of supporting conflict resolution is to teach and practise using a peace path, as developed by Slavin (1996) which consists of five steps:

Step 1: Take turns to state your feelings using an 'I' message:

I feel . . . when you . . .

I would like you to . . .

Step 2: Suggest a solution

Step 3: Restate the other's solution

Step 4: Agree a solution

Step 5: Depart in peace

Pupils can be trained to act as playground monitors to support others with the peace path and provide cool off times where needed.

KEY LEARNING POINTS

Phase 4 has examined the skills needed to work cooperatively. Key points include:

- Considering the types of skills, either *task skills* or *working relationship skills.*
- Teaching the skills explicitly in steps.
- Examining procedures for dealing with conflict.

Phase 5: Using a range of structures

There are a wide variety of structures, or cooperative learning strategies, that can be used in the classroom. Kagan (1994, 2009) has developed approximately 200 structures that can be used for a range of different lessons and subjects (see www.kaganonline.com). One of the key aspects about structures is that they are content free and can be adapted to suit any lesson. Appendix 1 provides a list of structures, which is divided into those that are fairly simple to introduce in lessons and those that are more complex once pupils are more used to working cooperatively.

One popular structure called **numbered heads** ensures individual accountability, as anyone in a team can be called on to give their team's answer. It works as follows:

- Pupils are grouped into teams of four or five pupils.
- Each group numbers off so that each person has a number (1, 2, 3, 4, etc.)
- Each group can also be given a collective number or letter.
- The teacher poses a question for groups to consider, often for reinforcement or checking understanding.
- Pupils discuss and aim to come to a consensus about the answer.
- The teacher reminds them that anyone can be called to answer for the team, so they need to be sure that everyone is ready.
- The teacher then selects a number and chooses a team. A spinner can be used to do this, or a dice.
- The pupil with that number has to stand and give their team's answer.
- The process can be repeated with different questions.

Ten popular structures and examples of how to include them in lessons are provided in Figure 3.5.

The key point to remember is that using structures will not guarantee successful cooperative learning unless positive interdependence and individual accountability are ensured to enhance equal participation. Structures are useful tools to develop cooperation and while using a variety of these is useful, it is not about knowing a huge number, but instead using them appropriately. A range of structures can be found in Appendix 1. There are also a number of websites that can provide information and free resources about using structures. See: http://cooperativelearningresources.weebly.com/structures.html.

You will also find a range of useful ideas and visual images on structures at Pinterest:

https://uk.pinterest.com/sglanz/kagan-strategies.

Structure	Explanation	How it is used
1. Think/pair/share* 	1. Teacher asks a question. 2. Pupils are given time think about it individually. 3. They discuss their answer with a partner. 4. When asked by the teacher, pairs share their answers with the class.	Used at key points such as during teacher exposition to help clarify thinking and to provide interaction with pupils. Important that questions used are open-ended and this structure is not over-used in a lesson. This can be adapted to 'timed talking' where pairs are given specific amounts of time to talk which helps ensure equal participation.
2. Round Robin 	1. Teacher asks a multi-answer question (e.g. how many words can you find to describe a picture). 2. Pupils are grouped in 3s, 4s or 5s. 3. Pupils either write or say their answers, taking turns round the group, passing a paper if writing. 4. The class discusses different answers.	This is used for brainstorming any topic. It can be useful to pre-test what pupils know about a topic. It can also be to review what has been recalled from a previous lesson.
3. Showdown	1. Pupils are divided into groups of four. 2. The teacher gives the class an oral question or problem. 3. Each member of the group writes their answer on an individual sheet. 4. When the teacher says, 'SHOWDOWN' each member of the group displays their answer to the rest of the group and they compare and verify their answers.	This is best used with short answers so that it can progress quickly. This can be adapted with a set of questions on cards provided for each group. The team selects a showdown captain who draws each card and reads the question. Groups write an answer individually and signal when they are all ready. Showdown captain, says 'showdown' and members show their answers.

Figure 3.5 (continued)

4. Twos to fours** 	Pairs work together and then share their ideas with another pair.	This is a quick way of creating larger groups at spontaneous times during a lesson. It is useful for sharing and pooling ideas.
5. Two stay and two stray 	After working on a topic, two members of the team move to an adjoining team to share ideas. Pairs then move back to their original teams to compare and share information.	This is a very useful way of reporting back after an activity so groups share their products, etc.
6. Corners 	1. This involves posting different words, pictures, or statements, etc. on pieces of paper at corners of the room. These could be linked to a topic of study. 2. Each pupil is then asked to choose one that appeals to him/her and one about which they want to find out more. 3. Pupils go to the chosen corner and discuss the topic with their classmates who chose the same 'corner'.	Corners is a good way to get children or adults up and moving around the classroom as they engage in standing conversations around a chosen topic. It can be used to begin a topic or unit or as a review at the end of a lesson. Teachers sometimes use corners as sentence starters and prompts to for pupils' writing.
7. Windows (One and All)	1. Pupils work in groups of four. 2. With one sheet of A4 paper, with a rectangle, or shape, in the centre of the paper and four equal sections around the outside. 3. Pupils take turns to write their favourite item (food, game, animal, etc.) in each outside section. 5. Pupils discuss and write things they have in common in the middle.	This is a simple framework for discovering similarities and differences between team members. It can be used as a team building activity with the middle section containing what they have in common which can be used to create a team name.
8. Three-step interview 	1. Teams work in pairs to describe or explain something. 2. Their partner listens carefully and then they swap. 3. Each team member then explains to the team what their partner has told them.	This is a good team building activity but also supports active listening skills and can be used for recalling or checking on information.

9. Doughnut (inside/ outside circle) 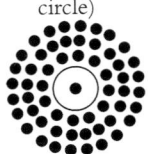	1. One-half of the participants stand and form a circle facing out. 2. The other half of the participants form a circle around (outside) of the first group, so that each participant is facing a person from the 'other' circle. 3. The teacher asks partners to introduce themselves if necessary, and asks a question for the inside circle person to discuss with their face partner. 4. The teacher instructs one circle to rotate, for example 'Outside circle move two persons to your right'. 4. The newly formed partners then respond to a question. 5. The teacher asks one circle to rotate again and then asks the outside partner to share what their previous partner told them and to add anything new. 6. Rotations can continue a few times to ensure maximum participation with different pupils.	This is a very useful activity for reporting, or for a plenary to a lesson to check on mastery of specific aspects.
10. Check and coach	1. Teams work on a class project which requires them to process material, e.g. to create a graphic organiser, poster, report etc. 2. The team needs to check everyone can understand and explain the work. 3. The team prepares a list of questions based on the project. 4. Team members pair with a member of another team. One pupil is partner 1 and the other partner 2. 5. They take it in turns to ask questions on the list and the partner tries to answer. The aim is to coach the partner to get the right answer.	This is for reviewing newly learned material and checking out understanding. It can be adapted with partners from the same team, or ad hoc partners, checking understanding using a list of questions. Pairs take it in turns to answer the questions with the other partner prompting and coaching.

*Source: 'Think Pair Share' by Giulia Maxwell (www.flickr.com/photos/gforsythe/26714165840/)
**Source: https://c1.staticflickr.com/3/2289/2137737248_e9f3e429d1_b.jpg

FIGURE 3.5 Ten popular cooperative learning structures

KEY LEARNING POINTS

Phase 5 has explored the use of cooperative learning structures. Key points include:

- Structures are cooperative learning activities that are content free and can be adapted to any lesson or subject.
- There are a vast number of structures, many of which are illustrated with online resources and videos. Ten common ones have been detailed here, together with additional ones described in Appendix 1.
- The key point is to select structures appropriately and ensure positive interdependence and individual accountability.

Phase 6 – Dealing with barriers to cooperative learning

There are a number of possible barriers that can arise to prevent effective cooperative learning. These can be categorised as cultural – that is, the school-wide culture is not conducive to working in this way. For example, senior staff expect classrooms to be quiet for the majority of the time, rather than talk being a central aspect to learning. Another barrier can be a lack of in-depth understanding by teachers as a result of limited professional development, or a lack of 'buy-in' to this way of working. A further barrier is the lack of skills by the pupils to work cooperatively. Linked to this is the issue of some pupils having specific behavioural or emotional difficulties that inhibit them working together. In summary, barriers are school wide, lack of teacher knowledge, or limited pupil skills or specific difficulties. This section will look at each of these in turn.

School culture

It is possible for an individual teacher to implement cooperative learning in a classroom, but it is difficult without a school culture that supports this approach. Chapter 4 will examine in depth the professional development methods and discuss the importance of leadership to create a learning community within classes and across the school that is conducive to cooperative learning.

Developing teachers' understanding

As discussed in Chapter 1, teachers need to understand fully what cooperative learning is and its key principles; the underlying theories that support it; what research says about the impact; and then reconcile this approach to their own beliefs about learning. This is clearly not a 'quick fix'. It requires sustained professional development alongside peer support. Further details are provided in Chapter 4 of how to accomplish this.

Examine Activity 3.2 which details some common issues that teachers cite. Where possible, discuss these with colleagues.

ACTIVITY 3.2: ISSUES NOTED BY TEACHERS IN USING COOPERATIVE LEARNING

1. *There isn't enough time* – teachers are concerned about the curriculum they have to teach and assess, and feel this could detract by taking considerable time to implement.
2. *I don't know where to start* – cooperative learning is a vast area with many different types and structures. This can be very daunting for teachers at first.
3. *Does this mean I have to revise all the lessons I teach?* – the huge amount of work that is implied by taking on a new approach is also very daunting.
4. How can I assess effectively if they are working in groups?
5. What about the pupils who just don't involve themselves?

You will find some suggested responses to these issues on page 135.

Developing pupils' skills of cooperating

One of the most common difficulties experienced is a lack of pupil skills. Phase 4 has detailed how to explicitly teach the skills of cooperating and the importance of developing these skills. These need to be practised with regular reflection, feedback and goal-setting, and where difficulties are experienced it may be necessary to revisit some of the trust and communication skills cited earlier.

Dealing with reluctant or difficult pupils

There will often be pupils who are reluctant to work in a group. Sometimes this is due to specific emotional and behavioural difficulties that require careful assessment and teachers will need support from colleagues, or specialists, in ways of supporting such pupils. Some pupils may have come to the class later in the year and missed some class and team-building activities and therefore they will benefit from peer support with careful pairing of pupils. Other common difficulties and some suggestions for overcoming these are given below:

- The **shy child** may find group work difficult and needs a supportive partner, at times working in pairs only. They need encouragement and positive feedback and their particular strengths identifying in order to make use of these in particular roles that are assigned. This helps build self-esteem. During reflection time, strategies such as round robin can be used to say something members of the group really like about another member of the team's contribution.

- The **free rider** is a child who lets others in the group complete the work. Here, making use of pairs where each has a key contribution to make helps. In addition, the use of roles in groups (see page 132) which are allocated to encourage everyone to participate and play to pupils' strengths can help. Jigsaw activities where each member of a group is responsible for a key part of a project can also be very useful in encouraging full participation.
- The **dominant child**. When a pupil dominates, ensure that groups are given different roles and one member checks that everyone contributes. Structures such as 'talking chips' can help where everyone is given a number of counters, or chip and to talk they have to place their counter in the middle of the table. Pupils cannot talk again until everyone has placed their chip in the centre.
- The **reluctant child**. If a child refuses to work with others, just let them withdraw temporarily. By observing the interaction of others over time, most pupils will at some point join in. Reinforce interdependence in groups by assigning roles and ensure that there are often fun warm-up activities. Have a focus for a week on everyone participating and reward different groups for this. You could also give a lone child a role such as roving reporter to check on groups' progress.
- The **rejected child**. For a pupil that is unpopular and who pupils are reluctant to work with, consider carefully the make-up of groups and place the pupil with supportive peers. Use group roles to encourage maximum participation (see Phase 9 for more information on roles). Use structures such as roundtable, round robin, three-step interview, and pairs check (see Appendix 1).
- The **high achievers**. Provide challenging roles and reward pupils for giving help and not giving the answers. They need help to see that there are benefits from working with others and that these are life skills.

KEY LEARNING POINTS

Phase 6 has examined barriers to working cooperatively. Key points include:

- One barrier can be the culture of the school, where senior leaders are not supportive of cooperative learning. It is possible for the individual teacher to overcome this but a cooperative school is a much more conducive environment.
- A lack of teachers' understanding of cooperative learning is another barrier. Professional development needs to address this over a sustained period and should include peer support.
- A further barrier is the lack of pupils' skills to work together and, as discussed in Phase 4, the teaching of task work skills and working relationship skills is vital.
- Some children have particular behavioural or emotional difficulties that make it challenging for them to work together. Some possible scenarios and solutions using cooperative learning structures have been discussed.

Phase 7: Phased implementation in lessons

Having an understanding of a phased implementation for cooperative learning is important, otherwise as one of the issues raised in the previous section highlighted, teachers can become overwhelmed with the huge variety of approaches and number of structures. This phase provides an overview of how to do this with examples, beginning with paired work. Figure 3.6 provides a summary.

Fernandez-Rio (2016) recognises the difficulty for teachers in implementing cooperative learning and has developed a cycle of three broad phases to support this process. These are: first, building group cohesion; second, cooperative learning as the content of the lesson; and third, cooperative learning as the framework, that is where groups are stable for a period of time. Fernandez-Rio (2016:6) makes an important point in considering such phases of implementation:

> The cooperative learning cycle is not a one-way structure. On the contrary, teachers can go back to phase 1 or 2 every time they believe that the group needs it. Furthermore, it is necessary to move up and down the different phases because 'rebuilding' group cohesion by using simple techniques is, many times, necessary to make progress.

Stage 1   Establish cohesive classroom and begin teaching teamwork and working relationship skills (this must be ongoing).
(See phases 1 to 4.)

Stage 2   Begin with small informal groups including pairs and trios, with simple structures and non-complex tasks.
Where appropriate, move pupils in 2s to 4s to work together for short periods.
Ensure positive interdependence and individual accountability.
Continue teaching skills.

Stage 3   Move to formal task groups for short durations with tasks with low academic challenge, and pupils grouped by random selection.
Ensure positive interdependence and individual accountability.
Introduce more structures.
Introduce reflection in groups.
Continue teaching skills including team building.

Stage 4   Continue informal groups and formal groups for parts or whole lessons where appropriate.
Introduce wider range of structures and increase complexity of tasks.
Ensure positive interdependence and individual accountability.
Continue developing skills and ensure reflection time.

Stage 5   Develop formal task groups further, including more established teacher selected teams for longer periods.
Introduce roles in groups.
Where appropriate use Jigsaw and other cooperative learning approaches such as Group Investigation and Complex Instruction (see Appendix 2).
Ensure ongoing development of skills with reflection and goal setting.

FIGURE 3.6   Stages in developing cooperative learning

Developing paired work

One of the first steps is to develop paired work in the classroom. This can be done beginning with very young children and works with any age. Pairs can be spontaneous, e.g., 'talk to the person next to you', or established as learning partners. Teachers may wish to start with spontaneous partners and where appropriate develop learning partners where children have been carefully paired, mixing ability, ethnicity, gender, personality, etc. to create successful pairings. There may also be opportunities for mixed age pairings, with older pupils coaching younger ones. The case study from India in Chapter 2 shows how pairings of children who have some form of disability with others can be very successful.

Consider the list of structures below and, if possible, discuss with a colleague which you might use and why, and how they support paired work. Appendix 1 provides a list of structures with explanations.

ACTIVITY 3.3: STRUCTURES FOR PAIRED WORK

Structure	*When it is used and why*
Think/pair/share	
Twos to fours	
Inside-outside circle/doughnut	
Mix-freeze-pair	
Hand up/stand up/pair up	
Pairs check and coach	
Think-pair-square	
Find someone who. . .	
Timed talking	
30 second speech	
Quiz-quiz-trade	

Moving on from paired work

Once pupils have become accustomed to working in pairs or trios, it is possible to spontaneously move them into fours (or fives where necessary). The structure 'twos to fours' can support this, or this is often known as 'snowballing' where groups grow in size. For cooperative learning, it is best to keep groups to a maximum size of five, as once groups become bigger the tendency is for them to sub-divide to smaller groups which affects the cohesion of the group. Working in this way with pairs or moving to fours, is all part of informal cooperative learning which can be easily incorporated into most lessons without significant preparation. The next section looks at planning for small groups in lessons.

KEY LEARNING POINTS

Phase 7 has examined phased implementation in lessons. Key points include:

- Consider the five-stage process beginning with establishing class cohesion, moving to informal paired work which smoothly moves into fours where appropriate.
- Ensure the teaching of cooperative skills continues throughout the process with time for reflection and goal setting.
- Move slowly into established formal groups.
- Gradually introduce more complex structures and approaches.

Phase 8: Planning for small groups

Decide on an appropriate lesson. Once you have explored some of the informal cooperative learning strategies and structures, you may wish to move into groups for whole lessons or series of lessons. Look for opportunities that provide some open-ended challenges or problem-solving that will help in providing a genuine reason for cooperating together in groups. As Phase 4 has examined in depth, it is important to ensure that pupils have begun to develop the skills to enable them to cooperate effectively, so it is worth remembering not to be too ambitious too soon.

In planning lessons for groups, you may wish to start with informal groups for a part of the lesson, progressing, when appropriate, to working in groups for most of the lesson. A number of decisions will need to be made to begin the process:

1. What cooperative learning skills are required?
2. How will groups be formed?
3. How many will be in each group?
4. How will the classroom be arranged?
5. What time will be needed for the group task?
6. What structures will be used?
7. How will resources be organised?
8. Will each group have roles such as gofer (resources manager), scribe, timekeeper, participation checker? (See Phase 9 for more information on roles in groups.)

One possible approach is to have a short part of the lesson where the pupils work in groups. A useful starting point for teachers is to plan a 'micro-lesson' – where possible with a colleague.

Assessing groups

An important aspect to be considered once groups become established in the classroom is how individuals and groups will be assessed. This is a common stumbling block for teachers. The aim should be to try and balance group grades with individual assessment. It is also important to remember, as Vygotsky (1934/1986:188) stated:

> What a child can do in cooperation with others today, he can do alone tomorrow.

In other words, the process of cooperating and working together aids the learning so that when a pupil does need to take an individual assessment or examination, they will be better prepared through learning with others.

Providing a group assessment supports team-building, for example when individual scores for an assessment are amalgamated into a group score. It is important to bear in mind the importance of involving pupils in the assessment – ensuring they understand the criteria and can assess themselves and peers against these. Clear success criteria, both for the academic content of the lesson and for the specific skill that is being practised, will help this. This is then considered in reflection time and goals set.

Johnson and Johnson (2004) have extensively reviewed assessment of groups and set out certain decisions that teachers need to make:

1. What is the purpose of the assessment?
2. What is being assessed? Is it the academic outcome of the lesson or the social skills or both?
3. What assessment procedures will be used?
4. Where will the assessment take place?
5. Who is being assessed (i.e. specific pupils/groups or the whole class)?

One these decisions are made, then the next step is to decide on the form of the assessment, in particular considering whether the assessment will be formative to monitor progress and inform the next steps in learning, or summative at the end of a unit of work to summarise achievement.

Ongoing formative assessment can be carried out as the teacher monitors the groups using checklists or noting anything particular to inform next steps. Assessment of progress is also a key part of the reflection that should be part of every cooperative lesson where pupils assess their own and group members' progress on the academic objective of the lesson and how well they are working together. From a student perspective, self-marking, peer-marking, activity evaluation and personal learning stories or logs are all proven methods of assessing collaboration. Research by Ross et al. (1999), with pupils aged 10, used a four-stage process consisting of:

(i)   involving pupils in defining evaluation criteria,
(ii) teaching pupils how to apply the criteria,
(iii) giving pupils feedback on their self-evaluations,
(iv) helping pupils use the evaluation to develop action plans or learning goals.

Task: to create a travel brochure setting out the most attractive places to visit in Wales and present to the class in groups.

Scoring rubric (1–5 with 5 being the highest)

1. Quality of information (range, relevance and clarity)
   1   2   3   4   5

2. Quality of graphics (range, relevance and clarity)
   1   2   3   4   5

3. Organisation (clear and helpful)
   1   2   3   4   5

4. Oral presentation (clarity and enthusiasm)
   1   2   3   4   5

5. Ability to answer questions (all members)
   1   2   3   4   5

FIGURE 3.7 Sample rubric

Assessment that is carried out at the end of a project, or unit of work, can be effective if criterion-referenced using rubrics. For this criteria for evaluating, work should be presented and preferably should be agreed with the pupils first to support ownership and their understanding of how to succeed. A rubric is a list of indicators of different levels of a criterion, using a scale ranking from poor to good (see Figure 3.7 for an example). They need to be tested and refined before being adopted. Pupils need guidance on using the criteria, which can be helped if to begin with they are fairly simple.

When groups produce a group product, then a group grade should be given. This needs carefully introducing, as some pupils may be concerned about the fairness of this at first. Examine the example below of a group score used for a spelling test and consider how effective you feel this would be and how such a process could be adapted for other areas of the curriculum.

Group scores: spelling test

This should be carried out as follows:

- Pupils in groups of four or maximum of five pupils.
- Begin by explaining that this is an individual test and ask them to write numbers 1 to 10 (or however many words you have selected) on a piece of paper. Tell them they are not to speak to others or copy others and should cover their work. Read out the words (these should be deliberately challenging).

- Put the correct spellings on the board and ask them to mark the spellings together.
- Ask the pupils to add up the total group score (appoint a scorer on each team for this purpose).
- Take in and display the group scores. Praise efforts and explain that these were difficult words. Talk about how some people are good at spelling and others find it more difficult.
- Now remind pupils of some strategies to learn spellings (such as saying WeDnesday and emphasising the 'd').
- Ask pupils to help each other to learn the words they got wrong and share strategies. Remind them that they will be retested and it is the success of the group that counts.
- After a defined amount of time to practise and help each other, re-test with each pupil undertaking the test individually.
- Mark as before and then take in the second group scores.
- Celebrate the success!

This form of group assessment is particularly useful at demonstrating the power of working together; as groups help each to improve their scores and individuals feel a strong sense of needing to try hard for the sake of their teams. It shows that assessment is an integral part of learning.

Another way to involve pupils in reviewing how successful groups are in working together is to use the **fishbowl strategy**. Here one group carries out a given task while another group (or the whole class) observes with them seated at strategic points around the room. This works best if pupils are given specific focus or questions to guide their observation, for example you need to check that everyone is participating.

One of the common concerns by teachers is that it will be difficult to assess individual contributions especially for a group product. Where an oral presentation is incorporated, it is possible to assess an individual contribution but for a written product, this is more complex. Possible ways of dealing with this difficulty involved:

- Conduct frequent assessments, or mini-assessments, so if a group is working on a project, at appropriate times, individuals carry out a short test, such as a short written explanation or quiz.
- Give random oral assessments, asking individuals to explain something to the group or the class.
- Where appropriate, ask the team to produce a team word web related to the topic. Provide each member of the team with a different coloured pen and ask each to make a contribution, signing their names in that colour on the paper.
- Ask each pupil to present the group report, or to make a contribution.
- Ask pupils to teach what they learned to someone else so that each group member presents a group project to another group.
- Assign roles such as a group checker where that person asks each member of the group to explain something (see pages 131–132 for more information on group roles).

One of the most important factors in making assessment effective in cooperative lessons is to involve the pupils, giving them ownership over what is being assessed and helping them to understand what to do to improve.

KEY LEARNING POINTS

Phase 8 examined planning for small groups. Some key points include:

- Decide on an appropriate lesson.
- Make a series of other decisions including: which skills will be needed; the group size; layout of the classroom; resources needed; success criteria; and if group roles are required.
- Decide on the form of assessment to be used and how pupils will be involved.

Phase 9: Developing longer term established groups

Once pupils have become accustomed to working together in groups for parts of lessons, or whole lessons, a further phase is to develop long-term established groups. It is important to ensure that the skills of working together are developing, although the reinforcement of these skills will require ongoing focus and revisiting at times. In establishing long-term groups the important factors are:

- Consider carefully the composition of the groups, making them heterogeneous (mixed ability, gender, and ethnicity), mixing personalities to try and avoid too many dominant pupils in one group, for example.
- Ensure that team-building activities are included to create cohesive teams.
- Ensure that lessons have both an academic objective and success criteria, and a skill(s) objective.
- Ensure that both positive interdependence and individual accountability are considered, as well as how these will be structured, such as the use of numbered heads, or two stray and two stay.
- Monitor the working of the groups carefully (e.g. using 'three sweeps') and praise those working effectively. You may wish to consider the use of team rewards such as points, certificates, etc.
- Ensure time is allocated for group reflection or processing to evaluate progress and set goals.
- If groups are not working well, discuss with the pupils and adjust the teams where necessary, moving pupils to another group.

One way to support the development of groups is to assign roles. Roles can help foster positive interdependence and teachers can assign roles so that every pupil has a task and must play their part. This also can alleviate any status issues, as discussed on page 34–35. Roles can help develop teamwork skills as these can be reinforced through teaching about roles. Which roles are used will depend very much on the age of the pupils and the context. Common roles include:

- Noise monitor: helps to keep noise within acceptable limit
- Note taker/recorder: writes down key information for the task
- Reader: reads the material to the group
- Checker: makes sure everyone participates and checks they understand the task
- Materials manager (gofer): collects all the materials needed for the task and returns them at the end of the lesson
- Time-checker: checks on time allotted and reminds members of time at key points
- Participation checker (observer): checks that everyone has a turn and nobody dominates.
- Summariser: restates or summarises a group's response or decision.

It is important to introduce the roles starting with one or two and adding more when appropriate. Roles can be allocated at random, but can work well, and play to individual's strengths, if the teacher allocates them. Roles can be taught in the same way as teaching teamwork skills using a T chart to define what they involve. Role cards can be used particularly for younger pupils to remind them of their roles, or alternatively badges can be distributed.

Teachers may decide on role rotation with pupils experiencing different roles. This may deter some pupils from dominating. You will find some useful resources for developing group roles at both https://serc.carleton.edu/intro-geo/cooperative/roles.html and https://mctcctl.files.wordpress.com/2014/09/cooperative-learning-member-roles.pdf.

KEY LEARNING POINTS

Phase 9 has examined the development of long-term established groups. Key points include:

- Careful consideration of the composition of groups.
- Incorporating team-building activities.
- Providing objectives for academic content of the lesson and specific team-work skills.
- Ensure careful monitoring of the groups.
- Provide group processing time.
- Introduce roles in groups.

Phase 10: Applying cooperative learning for different ages and different areas of the curriculum

In applying cooperative learning more widely, it is important to continually bear in mind the following key aspects:

- Ensure a favourable climate or classroom ethos so that a genuine community of learners is established. Pupils need to feel they belong and that they have a real say in decisions in the classroom.
- Start small. Remember that learning to work together is a gradual process that requires practice and should begin with some informal paired work building up to established teams, ensuring team cohesion is developed.
- Keep building and incorporate more complex activities, moving into formal groups where and when appropriate.
- Check the basic principles are incorporated of positive interdependence, individual accountability, group processing, small group skills and face-to-face promotive interaction.

These key points apply to different ages, although with very young children it may be better to focus on pupils working in pairs.

Once cooperative learning has become well established, teachers may wish to make use of more complex types of working. Appendix 2 details a range of these and some, such as jigsaw, group investigation, complex instruction and student team achievement division (STAD), are better used once pupils become more adept at working in cooperative teams. Activity 3.4 provides some scenarios. Working where possible with a colleague, decide which types of cooperative learning would be most suitable for each scenario. You will find some suggested answers on page 137.

ACTIVITY 3.4: USING A RANGE OF TYPES OF COOPERATIVE LEARNING

Scenario	Type of cooperative learning
Investigating the different aspects of a country divided into sub-categories.	
Maths challenges where team quizzes can be used to check progress.	
An open ended problem-solving activity.	
Assigning roles to groups to cater for all abilities and strengths.	
Investigate rainforests and make a group collage.	
Using peer support groups in the school.	

KEY LEARNING POINTS

Phase 10 has explored applying cooperative learning for different ages and across the curriculum. Key points include:

- Ensuring the foundations of good cooperative learning are established.
- Build slowly.
- Introduce more complex types of cooperative learning, depending on the age of the pupils, once they are ready for this.

Conclusion

This chapter has provided detailed guidance on the ten phases in implementing cooperative learning. As the case studies in Chapter 2 have demonstrated, in spite of the challenges in developing this approach, teachers from very different cultural backgrounds have had significant success in using cooperative learning. One of the aspects emphasised in the use of cooperative learning worldwide is the need to adapt it to work in the particular context. As Häkkinen et al. (2017:28–29) note, collaboration is challenging and teachers need to be well prepared as:

> Many things can go wrong in collaboration, and cognitive, motivational, and socio-emotional challenges may emerge.

They also state:

> If collaboration is not supported well enough and/or students do not have adequate skills, productive learning does not take place and students might end up with negative learning experiences.

(ibid)

The next chapter will explore forms of professional development and how to provide the level of support required for teachers to become confident and competent users of cooperative learning.

Chapter summary

You should now understand:

- the importance of carefully staged implementation of cooperative learning;
- details of the ten key phases of implementation:
  - Phase 1: Establish a community of learners
  - Phase 2: Classroom management and developing classroom norms of behaviour.

- o   Phase 3: Team-building
- o   Phase 4: Teaching the social skills
- o   Phase 5: Using a range of structures
- o   Phase 6: Dealing with barriers to cooperative learning
- o   Phase 7: Phased implementation in lessons
- o   Phase 8: Planning for small groups
- o   Phase 9: Developing longer term established groups
- o   Phase 10: Applying cooperative learning for different ages and different areas of the curriculum

- examples of application in the classroom, including assessment of groups;
- different types of cooperative learning.

Suggested answers to activities

ACTIVITY 3.1 SELECTING APPROPRIATE TYPES OF COOPERATIVE LEARNING

Scenario	Type of cooperative learning	Key factors to consider
In a history lesson, the teacher wants the pupils to check their understanding of a sequence of events that they have been studying.	Informal	This is a short activity where pupils need to check their understanding so talking to a partner would be appropriate.
In a history lesson, the teacher wants the pupils to consider the various causes of a major event, which they will present in the form of news reports.	Formal	Pupils need to work together to achieve a mutual goal which may take several lessons. Groups will be needed for this period.
In a history lesson, the teacher wants the pupils to examine two standpoints that provide very different reasons for a conflict.	Constructive controversy	This is an example of where dividing a group into two to present two viewpoints will enabled clearer understanding for a more complex task.
Pupils are studying a topic for a school term and need to form long-standing relationships to support each other's learning.	Cooperative base groups	This is a long-term requirement and needs established groups.

ACTIVITY 3.2: COMMON ISSUES NOTED BY TEACHERS IN USING COOPERATIVE LEARNING

1. *There isn't enough time* – teachers are concerned about the curriculum they have to teach and assess and feel this could detract by taking considerable time to implement.

    > *This needs to be addressed during professional development sessions. There are some underlying points here. The first is about coverage of the curriculum versus depth and helping teachers to understand that 'less is more'. Another point to note is that time spent in introducing this such as at the beginning of the school year, or term, is well invested in creating a cohesive and more productive class environment. It is important not to be too ambitious too early and start with some more simple informal activities as the pupils build the skills of working together.*

2. *I don't know where to start* – cooperative learning is a vast area with many different types and structures. This can be very daunting for teachers at first.

    > *Pages 118 to 121 in Chapter 3 provide guidance on how to begin with suggestions of simple structures and activities.*

3. *Does this mean I have to revise all the lessons I teach?* The huge amount of work that is implied by taking on a new approach is also very daunting.

    > *It will require re-thinking lessons that are appropriate for working in cooperative teams and again a gradual approach is best as the teacher gains confidence.*

4. *How can I assess effectively if they are working in groups?*

    > *Pages 128 to 131 examine methods of assessment but it is important to consider developing peer assessment.*

ACTIVITY 3.3: STRUCTURES FOR PAIRED WORK

Structure	When it is used and why
Think/pair/share	During teacher exposition to help encourage interaction with pupils and to check on understanding.
Twos to fours	An informal structure that can be used for short periods in a lesson when pairs can join with another pair.
Inside-outside circle/ doughnut	Usually in a plenary session to check on understanding and for pupils to report back.
Mix-freeze-pair	Useful to create random pairings to answer questions or share information at any points in a lesson.
Hand up/stand up/pair up	A random way of pairing pupils to share information.
Pairs check and coach	Pairs work together to support each other's learning.
Think-pair-square	Pairs discuss and then form a four.
Find someone who. . .	A way of getting to know different pupils or asking information from a range of different pupils.
Timed talking	To ensure that pairs have equal participation and both talk for allotted time.
30 second speech	To encourage pupils to have thinking time and to process new information. It breaks up any teacher talk.
Quiz-quiz-trade	A review strategy and helps pupils clarify their understanding of the content without the overly-used worksheet approach.

ACTIVITY 3.4 USING A RANGE OF TYPES OF COOPERATIVE LEARNING

Scenario	Type of cooperative learning
Investigating the different aspects of a country divided into sub-categories.	Jigsaw
Maths challenges where team quizzes can be used to check progress.	STAD
An open ended problem-solving activity.	Group investigation
Assigning roles to groups to cater for all abilities and strengths.	Complex instruction
Investigate rainforests and make a group collage.	Jigsaw
Using peer support groups in the school.	Learning together

References

Aronson, E. (1978). *The jigsaw classroom*. Beverly Hills, CA: Sage.

Bavelas, A. (1973). The five squares problem: An instructional aid in group cooperation. *Studies in personal psychology*, 5, 29–38.

Brody, C. M. & Davidson, N. (Eds.) (1998). *Professional development for cooperative learning: Issues and approaches*. Albany, NY: State University of New York Press.

Cohen, E. (1994). *Designing groupwork: Strategies for the heterogeneous classroom* (2nd edn). New York: Teachers College Press.

Cohen, E. & Lotan, R. (2014). *Designing groupwork: Strategies for the heterogeneous classroom* (3rd edn). New York: Teachers College Press.

Cordingly, P., Higgins, S., Greany, T., Buckler, N., Coles-Jordan, D., Crisp, B. & Coe, R. (2015). *Developing great teaching: Lessons from the international reviews into effective professional development*. London: Teacher Development Trust.

Fernandez-Rio, J. (2016). Implementing cooperative learning: A proposal. *Journal of Physical Education, Recreation and Dance*, 87(5), 5–6, DOI: 10.1080/07303084.2016.1156992

Gillies, R. M. (2003). Structuring cooperative group work in classrooms. *International Journal of Educational Research*, 39, 35–49.

Gillies, R. M. (2007). *Cooperative learning: Integrating theory and practice*. Los Angeles, CA: Sage.

Graves, T. & Graves, N. (1985). *Broken circles* (game). Santa Cruz, CA: Greeno, J. G.

Häkkinen, P. Järvelä, S., Mäkitalo-Siegl, K., Ahonen, A., Näykki, P. & Valtonen T. (2017). Preparing teacher-students for twenty-first-century learning practices (PREP 21): A framework for enhancing collaborative problem-solving and strategic learning skills, *Teachers and Teaching*, 23(1), 25–41, DOI: 10.1080/13540602.2016.1203772

Hennessey, A. & Dionigi, R. (2013). Implementing cooperative learning in Australian primary schools: Generalist teachers' perspectives. *Issues in Educational Research*, 23, 52–68.

Johnson, D. W. & Johnson, R. T. (1975). *Learning together and alone: Cooperative, competitive and individualistic learning*. Needham Heights, MA: Allyn and Bacon.

Johnson, D. W. & Johnson, R.T. (1996). Conflict resolution and peer mediation programmes in elementary and secondary schools: A review of the research. *Review of Educational Research*, 66, 459–506.

Johnson, D. W. & Johnson, R. T. (1999). *Learning together and alone: Cooperative, competitive and individualistic learning* (5th edn). Boston, MA: Allyn and Bacon.

Johnson, D. & Johnson, R.T. (2004). *Assessing students in groups: Promoting group responsibility and individual accountability*. Thousand Oaks, CA: Corwin Press.

Johnson, D. W. & Johnson, R. T. (2007). *Creative controversy: Intellectual challenge in the classroom* (4th edn). Edina, MN: Interaction Book Company.

Johnson, D. W., Johnson, R. T. & Holubec, E. J. (2013). *Cooperation in the classroom* (9th edn). Edina, MN: Interaction Book Company.

Jolliffe, W. (2007). *Cooperative learning in the classroom: Putting it into practice*. London: Paul Chapman.

Jolliffe, W. & Snaith, J. (2017). Developing cooperative learning in initial teacher education: Indicators for implementation. *Journal of Education for Teaching*, (advance online copy). DOI: 10.1080/02607476.2017.1319507.

Kagan, S. (1994). *Cooperative learning*. San Juan Capistrano, CA: Kagan Cooperative Learning.

Kagan, S. & Kagan, M. (2009). *Cooperative learning* (2nd edn). San Juan Capistrano, CA: Kagan Cooperative Learning.

Maslow, A. H. (1943). A theory of human motivation. *Psychological Review*, 50(4), 370–396.

McGrath, H. & Noble, T. (1993). *Different kids, same classroom: Making mixed ability classes really work*. Melbourne: Longman Cheshire.

Nguyen, P. M., Terlouw, C. & Pilot, A. (2006). Culturally appropriate pedagogy: The case of group learning in a Confucian Heritage Culture context. *Intercultural Education*, 17(1), 1–19.

Ross, J. A., Rolheiser, C. & Hogaboam-Gray, A. (1999). Effects of self-evaluation training on narrative writing. *Assessing Writing*, 6(1): 107–132.

Sharan, Y. & Sharan S. (1992). *Expanding cooperative learning through group investigation*. New York: Teachers College Press.

Sharan, Y. (2010). Cooperative learning for academic and social gains: Valued pedagogy, problematic practice. *European Journal of Education*, 45(2), 300–313.

Slavin, R. (1985). Team-assisted individualisation: Combining cooperative learning and individualised instruction in mathematics. In: R. Slavin, S. Sharan, S. Kagan, R. Hertz-Lazarowitz, N. Webb (Eds.) *Learning to cooperate, cooperating to learn*. New York: Plenum Press.

Slavin, R. (1996). *Education for all*. Lisse: Swets & Zeitlinger.

Stevahn, L. J., D., Johnson, R., Oberle, K. & Wahl, L. (2000). Effects of conflict resolution training integrated into a kindergarten curriculum. *Child Development*, 71, 772–784.

Thanh, P. T. H. (2011). An investigation of perceptions of Vietnamese teachers and students toward cooperative learning (CL). *International Education Studies*, 4(1), 3–12.

Vries, S. D., Jansen, E. P. & van der Grift, W. J. (2013). Profiling teachers' continuing professional development and the relation with their beliefs about learning and teaching. *Teaching and Teacher Education*, 33, 78–89.

Vygotsky, L. S. (1934/1986). *Thought and language*. Cambridge, MA: MIT Press.

4

PROFESSIONAL DEVELOPMENT APPROACHES FOR COOPERATIVE LEARNING

Learning objectives for this chapter

By reading this chapter you will develop your understanding of:

- the importance of teachers working together as a learning community;
- creating a suitable professional development programme for your context;
- factors in providing sustained support;
- using mentoring and coaching and lesson study;
- methods of review and reflection;
- working in networks.

Introduction

The most successful approach to implementing cooperative learning in schools is when there is a sustained and whole-school approach (Cordingley et al., 2015; Vries et al., 2013) as compared to short courses, which have limited effect. As Chapters 1 and 3 have emphasised, cooperative learning requires in-depth understanding of what it is, how it differs from group work, the theoretical and research-validated basis that explains why it is effective and how to implement it in a phased manner. Chapter 1 has examined the theoretical basis and underlying research that demonstrates the benefits of cooperative learning. In Chapter 2, examples of implementation in different countries have been explored, to help teachers through illustrating how cooperative learning can be adapted for different cultural contexts. Fullan, Hill, and Crévola (2006) argue that workshops, courses and related activities are often not powerful enough to alter the culture of the classroom and school, because they are not always linked to the context and, instead, provide external ideas and methods. It is hoped that the case studies provided in Chapter 2 will help schools to consider how cooperative learning can be adapted to work in different cultures. In Chapter 3, the ten phases of implementation have been explored in depth and it is hoped that this, together with the preceding chapters, will help form the basis of a professional development programme to develop cooperative learning in the classroom.

We acknowledge that effective professional development models:

> involve teachers as both learners and teachers (Darling-Hammond and McLaughlin, 1995), are needs-supportive (Aelterman et al., 2014), take place within the school day (Garet et al., 2001), are integrated into practice (Garet et al., 2001), are coherent with school and system policies (Desimone, 2009; Ingvarson et al., 2005; Penuel et al., 2007), and focused on transforming practice, rather than accountability (Kennedy, 2005).
>
> *(Bowe and Gore, 2017:353)*

This chapter will explore approaches to professional development with indicators from research into what works and why in developing cooperative learning. Recurrent themes from existing research that signpost what works in successful implementation include:

- The need for teachers to have a clear understanding of why cooperative learning works, (the research-validated theoretical perspectives) as well as how to implement it (Brody and Davidson, 1998; Johnson and Johnson, 1989; Sharan, 2010).
- The importance of connecting the values implicit in an innovation such as cooperative learning with the teacher's own beliefs, in adopting new methods (Brody and Davidson, 1998).
- Consideration of teachers' feelings of self-worth or self-efficacy as a new approach needs testing over time, gradually moulding it to an individual teacher's style. In this way a teacher gains confidence and competence (Cooper and Boyd, 1998).
- The value of teachers experiencing cooperative group work first-hand in any training (Rolheiser and Stevahn, 1998; Roy, 1998; Johnson and Johnson, 1998).
- The creation of collegial teams, or small cooperative groups, whose purpose is to work together to improve each other's success in using cooperative learning (Johnson and Johnson, 1994).
- The provision of sustained professional development which includes: different formal and informal learning experiences, inquiry and reflection, collaborative activities and ongoing support from an external facilitator (Armour et al., 2015; McLaughlin and Talbert, 2006; Goodyear, 2017).

The first three points above have been explored in previous chapters; the focus in this chapter is on creating a professional development programme to suit a context and how to establish sustained support. But first, it is useful to consider whether a teacher working individually can use cooperative learning.

An individual approach

Although a whole-school approach to developing cooperative learning is preferable, there may be teachers who have a strong desire to use cooperative learning in their classrooms even if they are not in a school where there is a commitment from everyone to do this. As Case study 1 from Annette, a teacher in England shows, it is possible to 'trail-blaze' and then inspire others in the school to work in this way. The key message is to learn as much as possible about cooperative learning and continue learning and to 'have a go'. To do this, as discussed in Chapter 3, five key steps can help. These are summarised below:

Stage 1: Establish cohesive classroom and begin teaching teamwork and working relationship skills (this must be ongoing).

Stage 2: Begin with small informal groups including: pairs and trios, with simple structures and non-complex tasks.

Where appropriate, move from pupils in twos to fours to work together for short periods.

Ensure positive interdependence and individual accountability (important for all stages).

Stage 3: Move to formal task groups for short durations with tasks with low academic challenge, and pupils grouped by random selection.

Introduce more structures.

Introduce reflection in groups.

Continue teaching skills, including team-building.

Stage 4: Continue informal groups and formal groups for parts or whole lessons where appropriate.

Introduce wider range of structures and increase complexity of tasks.

Continue developing skills and ensure reflection time.

Stage 5: Develop formal task groups further, including more established teacher selected teams for longer periods.

Introduce roles in groups.

Where appropriate use Jigsaw and other cooperative learning approaches such as Group Investigation and Complex Instruction (see Appendix 2).

Ensure ongoing development of skills with reflection and goal setting.

Planning cooperative learning implementation for a school: a staged approach (overview)

There are a number of key considerations in planning professional development for implementing cooperative learning.

- Developing the school as a learning community where there is a shared vision that includes equality, inclusion and democracy and a desire to use cooperative learning, where teachers and pupils are all learners.
- A well planned and organised training programme that utilises the expertise of one or more members of staff with additional external expertise where necessary. A suggested training programme is set out below, but it is important that this adapted to the context of the school and there are regular opportunities for review. This programme will need to be developed to fit the needs of the school, however, setting one day aside, while ideal as an introduction, is unlikely to be sufficient. Ideally this programme should take place over a school year with regular reviews.
- The designation of one member of staff, who ideally has more experience or knowledge of cooperative learning, to support others and ensure regular review at staff meetings of progress and consideration of next steps.
- Coaching and mentoring opportunities for staff. The use of Lesson Study (see page 147–148) can be beneficial here.
- Reflection on progress – opportunities for sharing what has worked well and any challenges experienced. The use of action research in the classroom can support more accurate and careful reflection.

ACTIVITY 4.1: SUGGESTED PROFESSIONAL DEVELOPMENT PROGRAMME

Set out in Table 4.1 is a suggested programme. Using this as a guideline, work with colleagues to tailor a programme for your school. You will need to agree the order of the programme, who will lead it and whether you will need external support, decide on how much time will be spent on each part, how staff will work in teams and how mentoring and coaching will be developed. The examination of case studies cited in Chapter 2 may also be helpful in considering how to adapt cooperative learning for your context. You will also find it useful to refer to the ten phases described in Chapter 3.

TABLE 4.1 A suggested professional development programme

Session	Theme	Professional development activities	Refer to
1.	Understanding cooperative learning.	What is cooperative learning and why does it work?	Introduction page 1–9
		Working in teams with example of ice-breaker/ team-building activity.	Chapter 3 page 110–112
		Create graphic representation of the five key elements.	Chapter 3 page 27–33
2.	Creating an inclusive and democratic ethos.	Developing class cohesion – reviewing activities	Chapter 3 page 103–105
		Use of class meetings and/or circle time	
		Involving pupils in decision-making.	
3.	Informal cooperative learning. Paired work.	Activities using pairs and trios, with simple structures.	Chapter 3 page 126
		Move from 2s to 4s to work together for short periods.	
		Classroom management signals demonstrated in training sessions.	
		Reviewing and agreeing norms of behaviour used in short group activities.	
4.	Teaching the skills.	Demonstration of how to teach the skills using one or two skills.	Chapter 3 page 113–116
		Examining a progression of skills and planning how to incorporate in lessons.	
		Opportunities for revisiting skills.	
5.	Formal cooperative learning.	Team-building experiencing range of activities and structures.	Chapter 3 page 127
		Working in small groups – experiencing group activities.	
		Importance of focus on objectives for academic element and cooperative learning skills and ensuring time for reflection on progress.	
6.	Barriers to cooperative learning.	Types of barriers.	Chapter 3 page 122–124
		Working in teams to review strategies and to devise others.	
		Conflict resolution strategies.	
7.	Planning for cooperative learning.	Planning for small groups – planning suitable lessons in teams.	Chapter 3 page127
8.	Long-term groups.	Developing long term established groups.	Chapter 3 page 131–132
		Group composition.	
		Group roles.	
		Assessment of groups.	
9.	Review and reflect.	Sharing successes and challenges.	Chapter 4 page 143, 147–149
		Involving pupils in reflection.	
		Mentoring and coaching opportunities.	
		Lesson Study.	
10.	Next steps.	Sharing a range of approaches and structures.	Chapter 4 page 148–149
		Action planning next steps.	

Sustained support

A carefully planned professional development programme is an important step in implementing cooperative learning. However, it is unlikely to be successful unless there is a mechanism for sustained support. Factors to consider include:

- Who will lead the development and what time will they be given to do this?
- Will teachers work in teams or pairs to provide mutual support?
- What time will be allocated to the training and over what period?
- Will there be external support?
- How will peer coaching and/or mentoring be set up?
- How will progress be reviewed?

Working with external experts, such as collaborating with academics from higher education, has been found to be successful. Goodyear, Casey, and Kirk (2014) argue that 'boundary spanners', for example, university-based researchers who cross their institutional boundaries to work with teachers in schools, need to support the development of school-based learning communities and can be helpful in supporting the implementation of cooperative learning and researching its impact.

According to Cordingley (2015:236) there are great benefits for teachers in participating in research-rich continuing professional development (CPD) activities including:

- improved knowledge of subjects and teaching and learning strategies;
- willingness to innovate and continue learning;
- improved confidence and skills in matching teaching and learning strategies with individual needs; and
- confidence in embedding strategies highlighted as high leverage by research in their day to day practice.

It is important that in any sustained planned professional development programme there is adequate time for engagement and collaboration with colleagues and that it involves active learning, reflection and a coherent framework to guide the improvement, such as the one described earlier in this chapter. As Bowe and Gore (2017:362) state:

> if professional development is to have more impact, we must not only respect the value of collaboration within local contexts, but also, crucially, support teachers to engage in the work of critically analysing and refining teaching practice.

Mentoring and coaching to develop cooperative learning

The terms 'mentoring' and 'coaching' are often used interchangeably and while there is permeability between the terms, it is useful to examine the differences. Mentoring is one example of embedding cost-effective professional development and if effective can build capacity in the teaching profession (Hudson, 2013). The relationship between mentee and mentor requires an openness to feedback and both should be willing to learn from each other in a reciprocal relationship. Mentoring is particularly effective when it is used for professional development, where mentees are observed teaching, and are provided specific feedback by reflecting on and deconstructing particular pedagogical knowledge practices, e.g. cooperative learning.

The last few decades have also demonstrated the benefits of peer coaching as a tool, especially when using the identified components of successful learning which include modelling, practice and feedback (Showers and Joyce, 1996). It has been found that teachers are more likely to implement new strategies when given the opportunity to work with a coach especially when employing the principles established by Knight (2007) that include equality, choice, voice, dialogue, reflection, praxis and reciprocity. Effective coaching should also include the following elements: 'content focus, active learning, coherence, and collective participation in ways that meaningfully bolster teacher and student learning' (Desimone and Pak, 2017:5).

CUREE (2005) in the UK developed a national framework for mentoring and coaching and distinguished between three types which all involve a sustained and structured process:

1. Mentoring – for supporting professional learners through significant points in their careers (e.g. from pre-service to newly qualified teacher) and usually involves someone more senior mentoring another teacher.
2. Specialist coaching – for enabling the development of a specific aspect of a professional learner's practice.
3. Collaborative (Co-) coaching – between two or more professional learners to enable them to embed new knowledge and skills from specialist sources in day-to-day practice.

Using the third type of collaborative coaching can be particularly effective in developing a new practice such as cooperative learning. It is important to develop the skills of coaching and this is often best done using a cycle, such as:

- agree the partnership and schedule (who, when and where);
- pre-lesson coaching meeting (focus and timing);
- evidence of practice collected through observation;
- post-lesson meeting – reflection, feedback and support;
- consider further coaching cycle.

Observing each other using cooperative learning in lessons will be beneficial both to the observer and the person being observed. It is important to be aware of the sensitivities of teachers when being observed. Keeping a positive stance is vital and to realize that the job of the coach is not to note everything that could be improved, but rather to focus on specific aspects agreed on beforehand. The person coaching/observing should remember to remain non-judgmental and just comment on actual events, etc. The key point to realise is that this is a reciprocal arrangement and peers are helping and supporting each other. You may want to consider using a tablet to record the lesson or part of the lesson, but this will need agreeing first and will depend on the school policy on recording lessons. The following guidelines can help:

1. Pre-observation conference: Discuss prior to the observation what particular area will be focused on. This may include particular pupils or any aspect of cooperative learning.
2. Observation: During the observation use an agreed proforma.
3. Analysis: Separately try to discern themes and patterns or attach significance to behaviours observed.
4. Post-observation conference: After the observation, try and discuss the lesson as soon as possible. Discuss what went well and agree steps to improve for future lessons.

Using Lesson Study (peer observation and reflection) for implementing cooperative learning

Lesson Study is a professional learning process. It originated in Japan and is used widely in the Far East. It focuses on the learning and progress made by pupils as their teachers develop specific pedagogic techniques and is ideally suited for developing cooperative learning. It is a model for collaborative professional learning where:

- two or more teachers work together, developing practice in the classroom, focusing on the needs and learning of pupils and trying to solve a teaching or learning-based problem;
- they are engaged in developing a teaching technique which is designed to improve a specific aspect of learning for identified pupils;
- they keep a record of what they learn and they pass on the practice knowledge which they gain to others – for example by coaching, leading a professional development meeting or providing a demonstration lesson.

During Lesson Study, two or three teachers work together and undertake the following:

- Examine data gathered from day to day and periodic assessment to agree a focus for the pupil learning and progress.
- Jointly identify a teaching technique to develop, or improve, which addresses that need.

- Identify three 'case pupils'. Each should typify a group of learners in the class.
- Jointly plan a 'study lesson' which develops the effects of this new technique and keeps in mind the three case pupils.
- Teach and jointly observe the study lesson focusing on the case pupils' learning and progress. They may repeat and refine this over several lessons or teaching sequences. Not all these steps need to be observed in every study lesson.
- Interview the case pupils to gain their insights into the study lesson.
- Hold a post-lesson discussion analysing how the case pupils responded to the technique, what progress they made and what can be learned for next time.
- Where appropriate, share the outcomes with a wider audience of other teachers.

You will find more guidance on lesson study from: http://lessonstudy.co.uk/what-is-lesson-study, including a free copy of the Lesson Study handbook. Lesson Study has been applied to cooperative learning, for example Marsano (2016) using Jigsaw with engineering students. The case study from Hong Kong (in Chapter 2, see page 69–72) demonstrates how this type of professional development can be effective in developing cooperative learning.

Participatory action research approaches to cooperative learning

Lewin (1946), coined the term 'action research' to include a series of steps of planning, acting, observing and evaluating the result of the action. In this type of professional development approach, the group studies some kind of improvement or desired change, and has decided on a thematic concern (Kemmis and McTaggart, 1988). This could allow exploration of cooperative learning in action in classrooms through reflection.

There is also a more critical type of action research: **participatory action research** or **PAR**.

> Affirming the notion that ordinary people can understand and change their own lives through research, education, and action, PAR openly challenges existing structures of power and creates opportunities for the development of innovative and effective solutions to the problems facing our schools and communities.
>
> *(Brydon-Miller and Maguire, 2009:81)*

Its purpose in schools has primarily been to improve and change teaching practice, support school reform and promote professional development.

Action research is both a participatory and democratic process bringing together, 'action and reflection, theory and practice, in participation with others' (Reason and Bradbury, 2006:1). It can lead to change in practice and allows teachers to apply professional knowledge in a cyclic way, taking responsibility for goal setting and changing these goals as they develop new knowledge. Action research is therefore a strategy teachers can use for empowerment, which can lead to changes in teaching practices.

This type of approach requires teachers to reflect on their practices, through collaboration and critique and often through collegial group meetings as a community of practice. Communities of practice are characterised by mutual engagement, joint enterprise, and a shared professional repertoire (Wenger, 1998). They involve those individuals who wish to deepen their knowledge and expertise about a shared concern, process or problem through ongoing interaction. In such an approach teachers are encouraged to make decisions for themselves and consider their own professional repertoire, driving their own action research projects deepening their knowledge of cooperative learning. A simple action plan, as outlined below, is able to be used to consider development and understandings of cooperative learning in the classroom.

Take stock of what is going on
Identify a concern
Think of a possible way forward
Try it out
Monitor the action by gathering data to show what is happening
Evaluate progress by establishing procedures for making judgements about what is
happening
Test the validity of accounts of learning
Modify practice in the light of the evaluation

(Mcniff and Whitehead, 2006:8–9)

As a result of critical and reflective thinking, and continual revision to practices, teachers can grow in their understandings of cooperative learning teaching and learning tasks/activities through such an approach. For an example of this in practice please see Ferguson-Patrick (2014). Early career teachers in this study developed and applied their professional knowledge in a cyclic way, taking responsibility for goal setting and changing these goals as they developed new knowledge (Kemmis and Wilkinson, 1998; Ponte, 2002). This reflective process occurred as each of the early career teachers gave critical thought to making changes in their cooperative learning lessons, and through reflection with others at professional learning meetings and, as a result of critical and reflective thinking, continued to revise their changes to cooperative learning teaching and learning tasks/activities.

Setting up networks and cooperative groups to support cooperative learning

Not only is it beneficial to develop a learning community in a school to develop cooperative learning, but also it can be helpful if links are made across schools in a network. There has been a significant interest in the potential of Professional Learning Communities (PLCs) as Stoll et al. (2006:221) note:

Developing professional learning communities (PLCs) appears to hold considerable promise for capacity building for sustainable improvement. As such, it has become a 'hot topic' in many countries.

Stoll et al. cite a number of factors that are encompassed by PLCs, including:

a group of people sharing and critically interrogating their practice in an ongoing, reflective, collaborative, inclusive, learning-oriented, growth-promoting way.

(2006:223)

The benefits of working in a PLC have been found to promote and sustain the learning of those involved (Bolam et al., 2005; Andrews and Lewis, 2007). A review of sustained collaborative professional development in PLCs (Cordingley et al., 2003) found that this led to greater teacher confidence and a greater commitment to changing practice and to try new things. Developing schools and networks as professional learning communities would therefore appear to hold much promise for the implementation of cooperative learning.

Jolliffe (2015) cites an example of one network of schools in England that had a key focus to develop cooperative learning. This network consisted of two secondary schools and eight primary schools, and the work was funded by the Network Learning Communities (NLCs) programme which was led by the National College of School Leadership and ran from 2001 until 2006. The schools in the networked learning community that formed the context for this research had a long history of working together and previously they had been part of an Education Action Zone (EAZ), a government initiative with the aim of raising standards and providing additional support in areas of deprivation. Even after the funding ceased for NLCs, this network continued to thrive and the research identified a key factor as the strong relationships that existed, particularly between headteachers (Jolliffe, 2011). The shared focus for the network was to impact on pupils' learning through the use of cooperative learning. By 2008, initial research indicated that over a period of five years, the central aim of implementing cooperative learning had been achieved. Questionnaires completed by teachers in ten schools, indicated a 100% (n = 97) response to the use of cooperative learning in classrooms, which included both informal paired work as well as more formal established groups working together, which is considered more difficult to implement. How this was achieved became the subject of further research. This study examined what was the impact of the network in implementing cooperative learning.

Results of this study obtained from interviews with senior staff and observations in classrooms showed that this network highlighted partnership and mutual support, and clearly indicated that the role of the network provided independence. In other words: the network provided the support to be innovative. Each school had an in-house expert, or facilitator, and the facilitator group which met termly proved powerful in the cross-fertilisation of practices, resources and a source of psychological support. The gradual implementation supported by in-house experts was crucial.

Observations were carried out in seven classrooms in different schools (Jolliffe, 2011) and they demonstrated in all cases that the skills of cooperating were developing. Pupils revealed a strong willingness to share in groups and they were observed mentoring each other. The case study discussed, provides an example of bridging the gap between the potential of cooperative learning and use through creating a network of schools working together, supported by a professional learning community of facilitators to provide in-house support.

IT networks

An example of more recent online professional learning communities can be seen in the synchronous discussion events held on Twitter where there is both interplay of personal learning with the more collaborative components of professional learning and practice (Evans, 2015). In Australia in particular, many individual professionals are expected to take responsibility for their own professional development and learning activities and many are turning to online forums and blogs where professional knowledge is generated through social sharing and they are refining ideas in such a community that has a common interest (Sloep, 2014).

Another professional learning community opportunity is called World Café (www. theworldcafe.com/key-concepts-resources/world-cafe-method) and was first developed by Brown and Isaacs (2005). World Café was not initially developed for schools, but is now a global conversational movement, with active participants and practitioners in business and organisational settings on six continents. World Café can occur in either an online (www.theworldcafe.com/tag/online-world-cafe) or face-to-face situation. During World Café the community comes together to explore a question that matters to them, for example how to implement cooperative learning school wide. The school would need to make the space where dialogue is to occur, hospitable, safe and inviting and encourage everyone's participation and ideas. They might invite community members to participate in World Café, as well as teachers and pupils. This brings together diverse perspectives in an environment where listening is emphasised as well as 'harvesting' themes and discoveries the group has made about directions the school might want to take. Graphic recording during the event helps to bridge the world of visual thinking and the World Café, for it helps to illuminate how people connect, contribute, learn and make meaning together. The use of Padlet (https://padlet.com/my/dashboard), an online bulletin board that you can use to display information for any topic, can be used to document the visual thinking of the World Café exploration.

This method of professional learning suits itself well to cooperative learning where listening and accepting other's viewpoints is a part of the democratic feel of a cooperative learning classroom. See www.theworldcafe.com/key-concepts-resources/world-cafe-method for some useful resources to support this method. This link provides a YouTube link to World Café https://youtu.be/1cv82Yl0H7M

and this one is a good introduction for pupils: https://youtu.be/7ODLvTBvKow?
list=PL8chxCQVSCEHGKIz4nEH7nc2fzYt1OAwE.

Conclusion

This chapter has explored approaches to professional development with indicators from research into what works and why in developing cooperative learning. While the most successful method of implementing cooperative learning is through a sustained whole-school approach, the chapter has detailed how just one teacher can put this into practice in their classroom. The chapter has provided an example of a professional development programme, but it is crucial for schools to ensure that any programme fits their context and needs. One of the aims of providing the case studies in Chapter 2 is to exemplify that one size does not fit all and that different approaches to cooperative learning can be very effective. Lesson study and mentoring and coaching also can be powerful as has been discussed. Above all, this chapter has shown the value of working collaboratively in teams and networks to support successful implementation. Virtual IT networks can also provide valuable support. Such support needs to be ongoing, as a cooperative learning classroom or school is always learning based on reflection and review.

Chapter summary

Having read this chapter, you should now understand:

- the importance of teachers working together as a learning community;
- the need to create a suitable professional development programme for your context;
- factors in providing sustained support;
- the benefits of using mentoring and coaching and lesson study;
- methods of review and reflection;
- the value of working in networks.

References

Aelterman, N., Vansteenkiste, M., Van den Berghe, L., De Meyer, J. and Haerens, L. (2014). Fostering a need-supportive teaching style: Intervention effects on physical education teachers' beliefs and teaching behaviors. *Journal of Sport and Exercise Psychology*, *36*(6), 595–609.

Andrews, D. and Lewis, M. (2007). Transforming practice from within: The power of the professional learning community. In: L. Stoll and K.S. Louis (Eds.) *Professional learning communities: Divergence, depth and dilemmas.* 120–132. Maidenhead: Open University Press.

Armour, K. M., Quennerstedt, M., Chambers, F. and Makopoulou, K. (2015). What is 'effective' CPD for contemporary physical education teachers? A Deweyan framework. *Sport, Education and Society*. Advance online publication.

Bolam, R., McMahon, A., Stoll, L., Thomas, S., Wallace, M., Greenwood, A., Hawkey, K., Ingram, M., Atkinson, A. and Smith, M. (2005). *Creating and sustaining effective professional learning communities*. Research Report 637. London: DfES and University of Bristol.

Bowe, J. and Gore, J. (2017). Reassembling teacher professional development: The case for quality teaching rounds, *Teachers and Teaching*, *23*(3), 352–366.

Brody, C. M. and Davidson, N., (Eds.) (1998). *Professional development for cooperative learning: Issues and approaches*. Albany, NY: State University of New York Press.

Brown, J. and Isaacs, D. (2005). *The world café book: Shaping our futures through conversations that matter*. San Francisco, CA: Berrett-Koehler Publishers, Inc.

Brydon-Miller, M. and Maguire, P. (2009). Participatory action research: Contributions to the development of practitioner inquiry in education. *Educational Action Research*, *17*, 79–93.

Cooper, C. and Boyd, J. (1998). Creating sustained professional growth through collaborative reflection. In: C. M. Brody and N. Davidson (Eds.) (1998). *Professional development for cooperative learning: Issues and approaches*. 49–62. Albany, NY: State University of New York Press.

Cordingley, P. (2015). The contribution of research to teachers' professional learning and development. *Oxford Review of Education*, *41*(2), 234–252.

Cordingley, P., Bell, M., Rundell, B. and Evans, D. (2003). The impact of collaborative CPD on classroom teaching and learning. In: *Research evidence in education library. Version 1.1*. London: EPPI-Centre, Social Science Research Unit, Institute of Education. Available at: http://eppi.ioe.ac.uk/cms/Portals/0/PDF%20reviews 20and 20summa ries/CPD_rv1.pdf?ver=2006-02-27-231004-323 (accessed 17.5.17).

Cordingley, P., Higgins, S., Greany, T., Buckler, N., Coles-Jordan, D., Crisp, B. and Coe, R. (2015). *Developing great teaching: Lessons from the international reviews into effective professional development*. London: Teacher Development Trust.

CUREE (2005). National framework for mentoring and coaching. Available at: www. curee.co.uk/files/publication/1219925968/National-framework-for-mentoring-and-coaching.pdf (accessed 17.5.17).

Darling-Hammond, L. and McLaughlin, M. W. (1995). Policies that support professional development in an era of reform. *Phi delta kappan*, *76*(8), 597.

Desimone, L. M. (2009). Improving impact studies of teachers' professional development: Toward better conceptualizations and measures. *Educational researcher*, *38*(3), 181–199.

Desimone, L.M. and Pak, K. (2017). Instructional coaching as high-quality professional development, *Theory into Practice*, *56*(1), 3–12.

Evans, P. (2015). Open online spaces of professional learning: Context, personalisation and facilitation. *TechTrends*, *59*(1), 31–36.

Ferguson-Patrick, K. (2014). *Establishing a democracy classroom: Cooperative learning and good teaching*. PhD: University of Newcastle.

Fullan, M., Hill, P. and Crévola, C. (2006). *Breakthrough*. Thousand Oaks, CA: Corwin Press.

Garet, M. S., Porter, A. C., Desimone, L., Birman, B. F. and Yoon, K. S. (2001). What makes professional development effective? Results from a national sample of teachers. *American Educational Research Journal*, *38*(4), 915–945.

Goodyear, V., Casey, A. and Kirk, D. (2014). Hiding behind the camera: Social learning within the Cooperative Learning Model to engage girls in physical education. *Sport, Education and Society*, *19*(6), 712–734.

Goodyear, V. (2017) Sustained professional development on cooperative learning: Impact on six teachers' practices and students' learning. *Research Quarterly for Exercise and Sport*, *88*(1), 83–94.

Hudson, P. (2013). Mentoring as professional development: 'Growth for both' mentor and mentee. *Professional Development in Education*, *39*(5), 771–783.

Ingvarson, L., Meiers, M., and Beavis, A. (2005). Factors affecting the impact of professional development programs on teachers' knowledge, practice, student outcomes and efficacy. *Education Policy Analysis Archives/Archivos Analíticos de Políticas Educativas, 13.*

Johnson, D. W. and Johnson, R. (1989). *Cooperation and competition: Theory and research.* Edina, MN: Interaction Book Company.

Johnson, D. W., and Johnson, R. (1994). *Leading the cooperative school* (2nd edn). Edina, MN: Interaction Book Company.

Johnson, D., and Johnson, R. (1998). Effective staff development in cooperative learning: Training, transfer, and long-term use. In C. M. Brody, and N. Davidson (Eds.), *Professional development for cooperative learning: Issues and approaches*, 223–242. Albany, NY: State University of New York.

Jolliffe, W. (2011). Co-operative learning: Making it work in the classroom. *Journal of Co-operative Studies, 44*(3), 31–42.

Jolliffe, W. (2015). Bridging the gap: Teachers cooperating together to implement cooperative learning. *Education 3–13, 43*(1), 70–82.

Kemmis, S. and McTaggart, R. (1988) *The action research planner.* Geelong, Victoria: Deakin University Press.

Kemmis, S. and Wilkinson, M. (1998) Participatory action research and the study of practice. In: B. Atweh, S. Kemmis and P. Weeks (Eds.) *Action research in practice: Partnership for social justice.* New York: Routledge.

Kennedy, C. (2005). *Single-case designs for educational research.* Boston, MA: Prentice Hall.

Knight, J. (2007). *Instructional coaching: A partnership approach to improving instruction.* Thousand Oaks, CA: Corwin Press.

Lewin, K. (1946). Action research and minority problems. *Journal of Social Issues, 11,* 34–46.

Marsano (2016). Development of a cooperative micro lesson study learning model to teaching creatively and teaching for the creativity of engineering students. *World Transactions on Engineering and Technology Education. 14*(2), 323–326.

McLaughlin, M. and Talbert, J. (2006). *Building school-based teacher learning communities: Professional strategies to improve student achievement.* New York: Teachers College Press.

Mcniff, J. and Whitehead, J. (2006.) *All you need to know about action research.* London: Sage.

Penuel, W. R., Fishman, B. J., Yamaguchi, R. and Gallagher, L. P. (2007). What makes professional development effective? Strategies that foster curriculum implementation. *American Educational Research Journal, 44*(4), 921–958.

Ponte, P. (2002). How teachers become action researchers and how teacher educators become their facilitators. *Educational Action Research, 10,* 399–422.

Reason, P. and Bradbury, H. (Eds.) (2006). *Handbook of action research.* London: Sage.

Rolheiser, C. and Stevahn, L. (1998). The role of staff developers in promoting effective teacher decision-making. In: C.M. Brody and N. Davidson, (Eds.) *Professional development for cooperative learning: Issues and approaches.* 63–78. Albany: NY: State University of New York Press.

Roy, P. (1998). Staff development that makes a difference. In: C. M. Brody and N. Davidson (Eds.) (1998). *Professional development for cooperative learning: Issues and approaches.* 79–99. Albany: NY: State University of New York Press.

Sharan, Y. (2010). Cooperative learning for academic and social gains: Valued pedagogy, problematic practice. *European Journal of Education, 45*(2), 300–313.

Showers, B. and Joyce, B. (1996). The evolution of peer coaching. *Educational leadership, 53,* 12–16.

Sloep, P. B. (2014). Networked professional learning. In: A. Littlejohn and A. Margaryan (Eds.) *Technology enhanced professional learning: Processes, practices and tools.* 97–108. London: Routledge.

Stoll, L. Bolam, R., McMahon, A., Wallace, M. and Thomas, S. (2006). Professional learning communities: A review of the literature. *Journal of Educational Change,* 7, 221–258.

Vries, S., Jansen, E. and van der Grift, W. (2013). Profiling teachers' continuing professional development and the relation with their beliefs about learning and teaching. *Teaching and Teacher Education,* *33,* 78–89.

Wenger, E. (1998). *Communities of practice: Learning, meaning, and identity.* Cambridge: Cambridge University Press.

CONCLUSION

This book has explored two key aspects that are fundamental to understanding how cooperative learning supports the intercultural classroom. These are:

What is cooperative learning and why is it important to support 21st century teaching in a globalised world?

How does cooperative learning support inclusive learning for all?

The book has strived to provide a balance of findings from research and practical advice of how to achieve this in the classroom. Teaching for the 21st century should enable our pupils to learn to address key challenges facing an increasingly globalised world and this book examines how cooperative learning is an inclusive 21st century pedagogy. In order to participate effectively in the 21st century, pupils need to have well developed intercultural understanding. To be able to communicate with others and learn to live together harmoniously is essential. Cooperative learning is a valuable tool to facilitate this. Teachers need to ensure when designing cooperative learning activities that they use the two key elements, which are essential for effective cooperative learning, these are **positive interdependence** and **individual accountability**. This will help pupils to build bridges with others and ensure equity and mutual engagement in an increasingly globalised world. This book shows the impact cooperative learning can have on inclusion to promote democratic classrooms. It demonstrates the improved academic outcomes that occur in a cooperative learning classroom, as well as an emphasis on supporting social emotional learning which enhances relationships. Cooperative learning can address inequality in classrooms as well as being socially supportive and inclusive.

Uniquely, the case studies outlined in the book, from many different countries and diverse cultures, provide concrete examples of cooperative learning in action in different ways. They demonstrate socially supportive and inclusive democratic classrooms. Due to the increase in high stakes testing in many parts of the world, particularly England and Australia where the two authors are situated, the case studies help to exemplify that in spite of such pressures teachers and academics are able to implement cooperative learning in different ways. Despite the factors that either support and/or inhibit the development of cooperative learning in these contexts, these teachers fully appreciate the benefits of this way of working and strive to ensure the implementation of it is sustainable. It is hoped that by providing a wealth of examples in different contexts, others will be able to see implementing cooperative learning is possible, regardless of culture or other national policy restrictions.

Boothferry school in England (the first case study), the third case study of a village school in Sweden using the storyline approach and the school in Australia in the tenth case study, highlight the great benefit of cooperative learning for developing confidence in their pupils' communication skills. The impact of cooperative learning strategies and pedagogies on English as an Additional Language (EAL) learners is stressed in these inclusive classrooms, with confidence of the pupils growing from dialogic talk, equal footing in circle time, the use of structures such as talking chips and the improved affective dimension to learning. Case study 11 about a small Aboriginal school in the Northern territory, Australia, also highlights the improvement and development of the pupils' social emotional learning skills. The fifth case study in Sweden, a school just outside Stockholm, also mentions the ability of new arrival pupils to be active, interact and bridge the achievement gap through using cooperative learning strategies in the classroom. The teachers in this school highlight the importance of talk and sharing of experiences for the children who may have fled war and may not have previously been to school. The cases continue to show us different inclusive child-centred cooperative learning classrooms and the way that pupils in these classrooms are more likely to show flexibility when working with different people, as well as be more accepting of people's differences. Case study 7 is of a small multicultural school in India, which has pupils with a range of disabilities as well as non-disabled pupils, and a diversity of castes and religions. The study demonstrates clearly how cooperative learning maximises the engagement of all pupils' engagement in learning, as well as the ability for all to express themselves openly, in such a supportive environment. Case study 8 in Singapore also discussed how cooperative learning has changed pupils' attitudes, especially with those who have special needs. Cooperative learning continues to be a pedagogical tool that demonstrates how pupils can support each other in a globally connected world and face the challenges that arise as a result of the diverse cultures that they live among today.

All of the case studies describe the ways teachers introduced and implemented cooperative learning in their contexts, and all outline the importance of the need to create a contextualised professional development programme for their particular context. Chapter 3 highlighted ways to implement cooperative learning in phases and examples of different types of cooperative learning in action were shown in the case study chapter. Case studies 1 and 6 both outlined their approaches to using the Jigsaw approach and Case study 9 is a great example of how to use Complex Instruction (CI) in the classroom. The small school in Italy has noticed that this tool ensured equal opportunities were given to all pupils, and the author of this case study describes it as a positive social justice tool. Case study 2, the cooperative academy school in England, demonstrated a way of using the Learning Together approach as they use Guilds with groups of pupils made up from all levels across the school, in a kind of peer support programme.

It is with sustained professional development that cooperative learning can become effective and is more likely to be sustainable. A range of professional development approaches are described in the final chapter, as well as a suggested professional development programme for schools, or teachers, interested in implementing such an approach.

We hope that this book provides valuable food for thought in demonstrating that cooperative learning is worth the effort involved. But to successfully implement this in the classroom, careful consideration needs to be given to supporting pupils and teachers in developing the skills required. Frequently, teachers have read of success in one setting and found it hard to develop in their own. We hope that this will book will support putting cooperative learning into practice through developing a deeper understanding of genuine cooperative learning and how to adapt it for diverse cultural contexts.

APPENDIX 1: COOPERATIVE LEARNING STRUCTURES

Structure	Explanation	Possible use
Think/pair/ share	Pupils have individual thinking time and then discuss an answer with a partner. They then present their ideas, or their partner's ideas, to the class.	To encourage maximum participation. Can be used for any content that is enriched by different perspectives.
Think/pair square	A/B partners share information around a given question or topic. Then each pair is asked to form a foursome by matching with another pair. The new group then shares information and synthesises the ideas of all four.	Encourages maximum participation and sharing of information.
A/B Partners	A > B Talk: Pupils take turns to speak in their pair in a more structured way, e.g. A speaks while B listens B then responds. B then speaks to A while A listens and then A responds to B.	To ensure equal participation between partners.
Talk cards	Talk cards are organised with one set for use with a group of four children, and each set is copied onto a different colour of card. The cards have letters A to D on each and numbers 1 to 4 with different pictures on two of the cards, such as animals. Talk groups are formed by children grouping with all	For grouping pupils and to encourage talk. The letters, numbers, pictures and shapes therefore enable the teacher to group children in a variety of ways.

(continued)

Structure	Explanation	Possible use
	children who have the same coloured card or the same animal or a different letter i.e. cat, owl or a + b pair. Each talk pair would then have a card with a different number or shape.	
Line ups	The teacher asks pupils to line up in any number of ways, such as: order of height, birthdays, alphabetical order, or it can be related to the topic of the lesson, and they line up according to how much they know about the subject. Each pupil then finds their place in the line. The teacher can then group pupils by mixing up those that know less and those that know more about a topic.	A line up can be used in a variety of ways to promote communication and to develop certain concepts as movement is incorporated into the day. It can also be used for grouping pupils.
Stand and Share	Individual pupils note something they know and something they want to learn about the topic. Pupils Stand up and Share and find somebody different to talk to.	Helps activate prior knowledge and provides opportunities to share.
Human treasure hunt/Find someone who. . .	Groups of pupils are given a worksheet requiring certain information that others in the class may have. They are given a limited amount of time to circulate and find the answers to their questions, filling them in on their worksheets as they circulate. After the time limit is up, pupils can return to their original groups of four and share any answers that others have not yet acquired.	Class building and getting to know each other activity.
Take off and touch down	Teacher asked questions and pupils stand up if yes to a question, sit down if no.	Ice-breaker and warm up activity.
Paraphrase Passport	Pupils pair up and decide who is A and who B. The teacher assigns a topic for discussion or a text to be read. Pupil A shares thoughts and Pupil B listens and paraphrases what Pupil A said. Pupils A and B swap and they share again in the same way.	Helps discussion in pairs.

Two truths and a lie (Find the fib)	Each team of four pupils is given a series of statements that relate to the topic, some being true statements and some being false. Through discussion, pupils try to determine the truth of the statements by referencing resources about the topic.	Can be used to check on understanding. Also a team-building activity.
Pairs check and coach	Pupils are paired by the teacher, or by random grouping. Pupils have a task(s) to complete and their partners are asked to coach each other to complete it successfully.	This can be applied to any subject where it is important pupils recall key information.
Listening triads	Working in groups of three, pupils take turns to be the speaker, questioner or recorder. The talker explains something, comments or expresses ideas, the questioner prompts and seeks clarification and the recorder makes notes and gives a summary at the end of the conversation.	Provides a role for each pupil in a triad which rotates. Helpful in reinforcing learning.
Twos to fours	Pairs of pupils join with another pair to make a spontaneous group.	Random grouping for sharing information.
One and All/ Windows	1. Pupils work in groups of four. 2. With one sheet of A4 paper, with a rectangle in the centre of the paper and four equal sections around the outside. 3. Pupils take turns to write their favourite item (food, game, animal, etc.) in each outside section. 4. Pupils discuss and write things they have in common in the middle.	A team-building activity with the middle section containing what the group have in common which can be used to create a team name.
Numbered heads	Pupils work in groups of four or five to coach each member of the group in the content. Once pupils have had group coaching time, they assign a number (1–4) to each member of the group. The teacher rolls a four-sided die or spins a four point spinner and that number of person is responsible for answering the question for the team.	To ensure individual accountability with pupils all ready to respond in a group.
Two stay and two stray (or one stray)	Pupils work on a task as a group of four.	A different way of reporting on a group's task or product and sharing with other groups.

(continued)

Structure	Explanation	Possible use
	At different times throughout the task, the teacher calls out 'One Stray' (or 'two stray' or 'three stray'). When this is called out, one or more pupils stray to other groups to borrow their ideas and bring them back to their group.	
Corners	Pupils in each group of four select a number from 1 to 4. Corners of the room are assigned a number from 1 to 4. Each corner group is assigned to discuss one aspect of the topic then return to their original group to report what they learned.	To find out more about a new topic and to process information.
Rally Table	Each pair of pupils has one piece of paper, or whatever the lesson requires, and two pencils. Pupils take turns writing, drawing, working steps of problems, etc. and then passing the paper to their partner who continues the next part.	A strategy that has pupils working in pairs to engage in processing new content or to practise a new skill. It works well for solving math problems; working one step at a time; constructing a paragraph or piece of writing; in science for identifying steps in a process.
Round Robin	Pupils are placed in groups of four, and the teacher offers a question or a sentence stem. The teacher then identifies which pupils will start the process, such as 'pupil A' or the pupil with the brightest coloured shirt. Pupils then respond to the question in a clockwise manner.	It encourages social interaction and verbal processing of information. It might be that pupils respond to a question, offer an idea, or complete a stem offered by the teacher.
Simultaneous round table	Pupils in teams of four. Teacher assigns a topic or question. All four pupils respond simultaneously by writing or drawing. Teacher signals time, or pupils place papers/pens down thumbs up when they are finished. Pupils pass papers one person clockwise. Pupils continue writing or drawing, adding to what was already on the paper.	As Round Robin.

All write Round Robin	Pupils are in groups of four or five and each pupil has a piece of paper. The teacher asks a question, gives think time. As each teammate says their short answer to the topic, each teammate writes the answers on own paper. Sharing continues in clockwise rotation until the teacher says stop.	To note each other's ideas and to focus on specific aspects.
Blizzard questions	In groups and each person needs 4–6 pieces of paper. They each think of questions on a topic or to get to know people better and write them on their pieces of paper. Pupils take turns to read a question and tries to respond. Timer is used to keep the activity short and focused.	Ensures everyone is participating and devises and attempts to answer questions.
Stand-up, Hand-up, Pair-up	The teacher asks pupils to Stand-up to obtain eye contact with another pupils and on signal go over to them and put their hand-up and then to 'high five' them. Pupils with their hands in the air, still need to find a partner.	This is a grouping strategy which provides pupils with a way to process information and share it with another pupil.
Three-step interview	Pupils discuss a topic using the following three steps: The first group member explains their answer to a partner. The partner explains their answer to the first group member. The partners team up to explain their collective answer to the other members of the group.	To support active listening to a partner and to ensure maximum participation.
30 second speech	This strategy gives intentional 'think time'. Pupils are given new information. In order for them to process this, the teacher, poses a question to the class and ask them to 'Plan a 30-second speech'. Pupils can jot down thoughts or just think about the question. Pupils are then paired-up and each person gives their 30-second speech to their partner.	To process new information and to break up any teacher talk.

(continued)

(continued)

Structure	Explanation	Possible use
Listen right!	The teacher forbids note taking for the next chunk of the lesson, (usually no more than 3–4 minutes). The teacher then asks pupils to work alone to make a few notes on what was just presented. Pupils are encouraged to write only main points in bullet point fashion, no complete sentences. Pupils then show their notes to their partners or group members, checking for accuracy and completeness. They can add points to their notes if their partner captured something important they did not. The lecturer then announces the key points and encourages pupils to add anything to their notes they missed. Pupils congratulate each other if they had all of the key points.	An activity for older pupils or adults.
Mix-Freeze-Group/ Mix-Freeze-Pair	Participants move around the room until the teacher calls 'Freeze'. The teacher then poses a question or sentence starter. Pupils are asked to 'group up' or find a partner and share their responses.	A class-building and content mastery strategy. This strategy can also be used to review content.
Doughnut/ Inside-outside circle	Have pupils stand in two circles around pupils from the other team so that the inside circle is facing out and the outside circle is facing in. Have the pupils stand facing a partner in the opposite circle and ask the first question, then have either circle rotate (e.g., the outside circle moves one spot to the right).	Useful for plenary sessions to reflect on learning.
Talking chips	Pupils are placed in homogeneous groups of four by the teacher. Pupils are assigned to discuss some issue and given a pre-determined number of talking chips to 'buy' their way into the discussions of the group. Once pupils spend one chip to speak to the group, they must wait until every other member of the group has spoken before they can spend a second chip.	To encourage equal participation.

Quiz–quiz trade	Pupils are each given an index card or a small slip of paper and instructed to write a question on the front of the card which cannot give a true/false or yes/no answer. Pupils write the answer to their question on the back of the card. Pupils walk around the room swapping cards until a given signal to stop. Pupils form pairs and ask one another their question, giving hints if necessary. Pairs then trade cards, and the process starts again and can be repeated several times.	This strategy is most often used as a review strategy and helps pupils clarify their understanding of the content without the overly-used worksheet approach.
Quick think (the minute paper)	At the end of a lesson pupils write on a slip of paper the most important thing they had learned and what content was least clear to them. Once they have written their thoughts, they can discuss with a partner or team.	Reflection
Roam the room or roving reporters	Assign pupils to teams. While teams work, one pupil can roam the room to gather information that might be useful for their team.	
Post and praise	Pupils 'post' a finished product from a lesson around the room. Groups move around the room in a prescribed fashion and write one positive comment on each, using a sticky note or feedback sheet.	
Gallery walk	Pupils (often in cooperative groups) have created a chart, constructed a graph, created a poster, brainstormed a topic, or developed a graphic organiser. Each group is asked to post their work in an area around the room. Pupils are then told to do a 'Gallery Walk' of the room noticing the thinking of each group. You may ask pupils to make comments and post them on sticky notes during the Gallery Walk or take notes for themselves as they travel around the room	A strategy that allows pupils to view other's thinking and works. It sharpens observations skills and serves to clarify pupils' thinking.
Whiteboard share	Following from team work, such as three-step interview, one representative from each team posts their best answer on the board or flip chart.	

(continued)

(continued)

Structure	Explanation	Possible use
The grid	Using a four-by-three grid for each pupil, with rows labelled such as, 'what I learned', 'something I did not understand', 'something I found interesting'. They fill in for themselves and find other pupils to write their thoughts.	
Graphic organisers	These are visual frames used to represent and organise learning information. Commonly used Graphic Organisers include: Venn Diagrams; Line Graphs; Mind Maps; T-Charts; Fish Bones; Pyramids; and Matrix Charts.	To process and organise information.
Diamond ranking	Teams are given a series of nine statement cards and then decide how to rank them in a diamond with the most important at the top.	
Jigsaw	The task is divided into parts, with each group member being given one part of the information to study and become 'expert' about. New 'expert' groups are formed to find out more. Once individual study is done, the experts join their home group and become the teachers to the rest of the group about their part of the topic.	This could be used for studying any topic that can be easily sub-divided into parts, such as an historical event. Each pupil in a group of four takes responsibility for one of the different aspects which they later have to teach to their home group.

APPENDIX 2: TYPES OF COOPERATIVE LEARNING

Type of cooperative learning	Brief outline
Learning Together, Johnson and Johnson (1999)	This incorporates three types of cooperative learning (formal, informal and cooperative base groups). Each cooperative lesson or activity should include the five essential elements: positive interdependence, individual accountability, group processing, small group skills and face-to-face promotive interaction (PIGSF). The whole school should be organised in a cooperative team-based way. This results in the routine use of cooperative learning with teachers supporting each other in resolving issues and developing its use.
The Structural Approach, Spencer Kagan (Kagan and Kagan, 2009)	This approach focuses on the key elements of positive interdependence, individual accountability, equal participation and simultaneous interaction, (PIES) and incorporates setting up teams and then using structures or social interaction sequences. These strategies, or structures, are content-free mechanisms and widely transferable across the curriculum.
Student teams achievement division (STAD), Robert Slavin (1994)	Teams usually consist of four members who are mixed in gender, ability and ethnicity. The teacher presents the lesson, and then pupils work in teams to ensure that all members have mastered the objective. Pupils then take individual tests on the material and scores are averaged for teams and compared with past scores, with teams rewarded for meeting certain criteria.

(continued)

(continued)

Type of cooperative learning	Brief outline
Group Investigation, Yael and Shlomo Sharan (1992)	A problem-solving approach which has four elements: investigation, interaction, interpretation and intrinsic motivation. It encourages higher-order thinking skills by comparing, contrasting and integrating a range of ideas, concepts and findings.
Jigsaw, Elliott Aronson (Aronson et al., 1978)	Each member of a group learns an essential part of a whole of a topic by working with a focus or expert group and then returns to the home group to teach this to others so that groups can combine the knowledge to complete the task.
Complex Instruction, Elizabeth Cohen (1994)	This approach aims to achieve equity in the classroom by recognising status issues and ensures that tasks incorporate various multiple intelligence factors so that all members of the class may have an opportunity to contribute.

References

Aronson, E., Blaney, N., Stephan, C., Sikes, J., and Snapp, M. (1978). *The Jigsaw classroom.* Beverly Hills, CA: Sage.

Cohen, E. G., (1994). *Designing groupwork: Strategies for the heterogeneous classroom* (2nd edn.). New York: Teachers College Press.

Johnson, D. W. and Johnson, R. T. (1999). *Learning together and alone: cooperative, competitive, and individualistic learning* (5th edn.) Boston, MA: Allyn and Bacon.

Kagan, S., and Kagan, M. (2009). *Cooperative learning* (2nd edn.). San Juan Capistrano, CA, Kagan Cooperative Learning.

Sharan, Y., and Sharan, S. (1992). *Expanding cooperative learning through group investigation.* New York: Teachers College Press.

Slavin, R. E. (1994). *Using Student Team Learning* (2nd edn.). Baltimore, MD: Johns Hopkins University, Center for Social Organization of Schools.

INDEX